The Experts Greet the
New Marketing Conversation

Throw out the old marketing paradigms! Today, marketing success demands that you engage the customer, and this book takes this concept to the next level with the roadmap on how to do it. Learn the art and science of winning marketing strategies that will ensure all touchpoints in your conversation achieve your objectives, deliver results, and build your brand.

Reggie Brady, President
Reggie Brady Marketing Solutions

This book provides concrete examples and a detailed work plan to achieve marketing success while remembering the all-important Return On Investment. *Marketing Conversations* will keep you conversing for years.

Richard Goldsmith, Chairman
The Horah Group
Author, *Direct Mail for Dummies*

When you meet someone and let him or her do the talking and you just listen, they'll usually leave thinking, 'that person is a great conversationalist.' Research backs that up and in marketing today the same practice applies. People are bombarded by some 600 contacts a day and are apt to respond best to those who they know care and listen. Donna Baier Stein and Alexandra MacAaron get it and with *The New Marketing Conversation* they offer a welcome and needed guide to starting a conversation with your customers that lets them take the lead. Read this book and learn how to use multiple channels to let customers know you're listening and how to accommodate changing tastes and trends instead of crafting them.

Jon Gordon
E-Commerce Copywriter
Target Corporation

Donna Baier Stein's and Alexandra MacAaron's *The New Marketing Conversation* is the definitive primer on direct marketing.

Denny Hatch
Denny Hatch Associates, Inc.
Author, *Million Dollar Mailings* and
Contributing Editor to *Target Marketing Magazine*

Solid theory and proven practice . . . all in one informative volume.

If your budget allows only one book in your marketing library this must be it. In it you'll learn how the basic direct marketing principles apply across a broad spectrum of today's marketing channels—direct mail, radio, TV, the Web, newsletters, telemarketing, email and wireless. Before you write even one word make sure to look carefully at the chapters on developing a communications strategy and the "media of conversation." It's in these critical early thinking stages that a marketing campaign is often won or lost. And, because the authors are two solid practicing direct marketing professionals they give you the specifics on how to put their proven principles to work.

Roland Kuniholm
Senior Associate for Membership
National Wildlife Federation

The era of preaching to prospects is over. Engaging consumers in mutually beneficial dialogues is the new reality . . . and *The New Marketing Conversation* is a lively and insightful road map to this emerging strategy. Donna Baier Stein and Alexandra MacAaron have not predicted the future; they have simply looked farther ahead than most people and seen the inevitable next-step in the evolution of marketing. A must read for anyone who wants to reach America's ever-increasingly sophisticated consumers.

Willis Turner
Senior Writer
Huntsinger & Jeffer

The NEW Marketing Conversation

Creating and Strengthening Relationships Between Buyers and Sellers

DONNA BAIER STEIN
ALEXANDRA MACAARON

Australia • Canada • Mexico • Singapore • Spain • United Kingdom • United States

The NEW Marketing Conversation:
Creating and Strengthening Relationships Between Buyers and Sellers
Donna Baier-Stein and Alexandra MacAaron

ISBN: 0-324-20057-9
Printed and bound in the United States by Phoenix Book Technology
1 2 3 4 5 6 7 8 9 07 06 05 04

For more information, contact Texere at Thomson Higher Education, 5191 Natorp Boulevard, Mason, Ohio, USA 45040. You can also visit our website at www.thomson.com/learning/texere.

This publication is designed to provide accurate and authoritative information in regard to the subject matter covered. It is sold with the understanding that the publisher is not engaged in rendering legal, accounting or other professional services. If legal advice or other expert assistance is required, the services of a competent professional person should be sought.

Consulting Editor in Marketing: Richard A. Hagle
Composition by Sans Serif, Inc.

This book is printed on acid-free paper.

With love to my main conversational partners—
Dad, Mom, Larry, Jon and Sarah.

DBS

For Maddie and Jim.

Thanks for all the love and support . . . and for staying out of Mommy's office when she's writing. x x x

AM

Contents

Acknowledgements

I'd like to thank Martin Baier, DMA Hall of Famer and #1 father, for first instilling a love of direct marketing in me. His intelligence and passion for this industry are unmatched, and I know that his many grateful students and colleagues echo that praise. The truth is that all things new build on past wisdom. Not only my father but Bob Stone, Joan Throckmorton, Hank Burnett, Bill Jayme, Stan Rapp, Tom Collins, Alice Zea, Les Wunderman, Pete Hoke, Dick Hodgson, Dick Benson, Max Ross, Jerome Hardy, Joan Manley, Rose Harper, John Jay Daly, Lu Daly, and so many others have helped make today's new marketing conversations as exciting as they are.

In addition to these people who were heroes to me growing up, I'd also like to thank the best friends I've made in this business: M. Virginia (Ginny) Daly and Kate Petranech. You are both true blessings in my life.

My sincere gratitude to Marla Hoskins of The Response Shop for taking time from her busy agency work to lend her considerable expertise to the writing of the chapter on television . . . to Jean Hall (one of the very best copywriters I know) for lending her writing skills and knowledge to the chapter on radio . . . Marilyn Ewer for her expertise on newsletters both on- and off-line . . . and to Margaret Maloney for bringing her excellent editorial skills to every chapter. Rich Hagle, our main editor, is someone who's worked tirelessly to keep the direct marketing conversation alive and well. From his immensely successful editing and preparation of Bob Stone's *Successful Direct Marketing Methods* to *Contemporary Database Marketing* by Martin Baier, Kurt Ruf and Goutam Chakraborty. . . . Rich has helped publish the best titles in the industry. It has been an honor to work with him, and I thank him personally for his kind patience with my busy schedule.

Thank you to the talented and hard-working Floyd Kemske, Doug

Hamer, and Cynthia Brown—all three mainstays of my business. Thank you to my mother for her love, support, and patience and to my husband Larry and our wonderful children Jon and Sarah—for everything.

Donna Baier Stein

Over the years, I've had the honor of engaging in a very fruitful "marketing conversation" with some of the best and brightest in our industry. My thanks to Jerry Mosier, Joe Cappadona, Rick Sperry, Steve Bouchard, Ted Livingston, Linda Maslin, Carol Thieman, Ted Leonsis, Diane Staley, Bob Kasper, Paul Berenson, Carolynn Isham, Jim Rosenberg, Jim Hackett, Phin Gay, Frank Papsadore, Hank Riner, Alan Rosenspan, 20 years of great clients, everyone at NEDMA and, most importantly, my beloved drones at Plan B. I'd like to thank Meridee Stein, Vicky Blumenthal and Olga Talyn who taught me about commitment, dedication, responsibility and how to play well with others. Thanks to my many supportive and brilliant and creative friends. Thanks to all my families . . . in New York, Marblehead and Columbus. Thanks to my editors, Rich and Margaret. And, I especially thank my coauthor Donna Baier Stein who has been an inspiration as long as I've known her.

Alex MacAaron

I

Marketing Conversations

The New Marketing Conversation

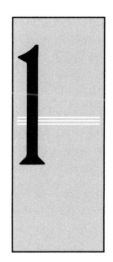

Marketing messages have certainly been around a long time. Throughout the last century, "new media" have been added to the marketing mix with exciting regularity: not just print, but telephone, radio, television, the Internet, and wireless Personal Digital Assistants (PDAs) to name a few. Each of these new media added to the number of opportunities advertisers had to reach their target audience. Today, as marketing conversations take place in all these media, the growth of integrated media marketing outpaces total economic growth.

For instance, direct marketing, the best example of integrated media marketing, is forecast to become increasingly efficient, with sales projected to grow steadily. Sales revenue attributable to integrated direct marketing is estimated to grow by 9.6 percent annually to reach $2.7 trillion by 2005. While each segment of the integrated marketing industry can expect healthy, steady growth, interactive sales alone are expected to grow by 41.3 percent per year to reach $136.4 billion in 2005.[1]

What's more, integrated media marketing advertising expenditures already represent more than half—56.5 percent—of total U.S. advertising expenditures.

With these kinds of statistics, it's not surprising that today, at least in the United States, there are few places you can visit where you won't be bombarded with advertising messages.

You'll find them on the pump at your local gas station, on the display screen of your neighborhood ATM, and in pop-ups, cookies, and banner announcements on your own personal computer screen. Marketing messages fill your newspaper, shout at you from the movie screen at the multiplex, and sing to you from your car radio. It's estimated that the average American citizen is exposed to something like six hundred marketing messages per day!

Think about that for a moment. You may be a professional marketer, but you're also a consumer. As a consumer, you too are the target and recipient of those six hundred daily advertising messages. Be candid. What do you think about them? Do they annoy you? Do they interrupt your thought processes? Intrude on your personal, dinner table conversations? Disturb your concentration at work? You're a rare individual if you can't answer "yes" to some—or all, of the above questions!

Now think about the ads that don't annoy you. What is it that makes them stand out in your mind? What about them captures your attention? Why do they seem worthwhile to you?

The answer is in the word "you." If these messages seem to speak to you as an individual, they become memorable. If an ad addresses a need you feel in your own life, if it offers a product or service that you view as either necessary or pleasurable, then you're likely to respond to it. In responding, you acknowledge its "rightness," its value to you, and so you remember it.

In other words, a successful marketing message relates to you, the consumer, and engages you in a mental conversation.

A major task for marketers in the coming years will be to create and implement engaging marketing conversations that are effective and that generate profit. A second task will be to help create conversations that are two-way and mutually beneficial.

Let's begin with that first, all-important task: creating effective, profit-generating advertising messages. To reach that goal, we'll show you how to generate consistently effective integrated media marketing conversations—conversations that turn prospects into buyers.

The vehicles by which you may reach your customer and/or prospect are varied. One of the most important things you as an integrated media marketer must remember is that a connecting thread ties these vehicles together. Whether your message is delivered via print, phone, the Internet, television, radio, or wireless PDAs ultimately makes no difference. These media are all potentially effective marketing tools, but, they are just that, tools. The purpose of the message remains all-important, and that purpose is to attract, cultivate, and retain buyers. With an ever increasing choice of marketing media, where do you begin? You must start by embracing the concept of *the new marketing conversation*.

The Marketing Conversations

Picture yourself at a dinner party. You are seated between two people you have never met before. Both are attractive, intelligent, and well-spoken.

The person to your right introduces himself and starts talking. He doesn't stop to ask if what he is talking about is of interest to you. In fact, he doesn't let you get a word in edgewise. He is engaged in his topic, so he assumes you are. When you do manage to ask a question, he either ignores it or rushes through an answer in order to get back to his monologue. You get the sense that there might be something interesting in what he's saying, but he hasn't given you a chance to find out for sure.

Now, the person to your left introduces herself. She tells you a little about herself, but she also asks you some questions about your family, what you do for a living, and where you're from. She asks if you're interested in something and waits until you affirm that you are before sharing her perspective on it. She stops talking frequently to allow you to contribute. She listens attentively and answers your questions. She actually shifts her train of thought in response to what you've shown interest in.

With which guest would you rather converse? With whom would you rather reconnect at a later date?

The problem with so much marketing is that while it may attempt to engage the customer or prospect, it's really taking the role of the first person we've just described. Even committed integrated marketers, professionals who champion the concept of two-way communication, spend most of their time, effort, and money talking about their own product or service. Too often, marketers don't listen—and that means that consumers won't listen either.

Historically, the advertising industry operated under a gross misconception—if we build it, they will come. This is not necessarily true anymore. Advertise and they may come, but they may not.

Most mass messages no longer work as stand-alone vehicles. In fact, the consumers of today, and especially tomorrow, will be able to "tune-out" your marketing messages. They can do so using technology, like online ad blocking, caller i.d., e-mail filters, and interactive TV. And even without these tools, they certainly will ignore your messages as they multitask through their ever more fragmented and complicated lives.

Gone are the days when the family sat around one television set rapt with attention. Today's family is more likely to be receiving hundreds of concurrent messages via dozens of media and devices.

What about so-called "targeted marketing?" It was certainly an improvement and has been a highly effective strategy for decades, but it didn't encourage the idea of building a relationship. After all, you're not likely to have much of a relationship with someone who's hunting you. What about a long-term commitment? There's none implied at all.

Integrated marketing became the industry's *cause celebre* about twenty years ago. And again, it represented an improvement. A consistent message delivered over a variety of media vehicles did increase awareness and response. Yet, even these efforts were usually limited to one, multimedia, message (and that one most often a message about the marketer's product, not the customer's needs). These marketing programs were rarely designed to start, build, and nurture ongoing customer relationships.

It's Time for a New Approach

Why now? Today's consumer is adept at reviewing, considering, and, too often ignoring, the bombardment of media messages he or she receives each day. In fact, more and more consumers are putting themselves in control of when, how, and where they go for the information they need to make a purchase decision.

Consider a person who is looking for a new car. He is exposed to mass media advertising on television billboards, and print ads in major publications, and may form some brand preferences based on those experiences He goes online to research the product attributes of a particular vehicle using both the manufacturer's web site and independent resources like *Consumer Reports*. He hears radio spots for the local dealership and checks the Sunday newspaper for current special offers. Once he has purchased his new vehicle, he receives direct mail reminders and opts-in for e-mail service offers.

Buying a new car is a carefully considered purchase for most people. Consumers are driving the same kinds of multimedia interactions across many categories, from high-ticket business-to-business (B2B) purchases, to furniture, running shoes, baby products, books, and CDs. To make matters more complicated for marketers, each individual consumer has his or her own preferences as to which channel they want to use, and when. Some people focus on just one medium; for example, they may browse, research, and purchase online. Most use some combination that fits their schedule, comfort level, and preferences. As a marketer, it's important that you recognize this and pay close attention to what consumers say they want, and to what they actually do. While consumers will cite channel or media preference, the reality is that most consumers use, respond to, and interact with a rich mix of media.

The integrated marketing approach would suggest that marketers must ensure that these consumers see, hear, and experience a consistent brand message across each of these many media. Consistency is only the beginning however, and, asking for feedback or a response is not sufficient anymore. *Today, you need to build an ongoing conversation.* The new marketing conversation is the next step in an evolution from one-way and two-way communication. Here's why.

The Fine Art of Really Conversing with Your Customers As a marketer, you need to introduce yourself to your prospects and customers, pique their interest, attain their permission to speak, listen—really listen—and speak again. The customer will tell you how and how often they want you to contact them. Again, think of rich and satisfying conversations. What are some of the attributes they share?

Getting to Know Your Prospects and Customers

When you've been introduced to a new person, there is usually a bit of formality involved. Even in a casual setting, people rarely share their deepest and darkest secrets with someone they've just met. Polite preliminaries are needed in marketing as well as in personal conversations. You must earn the prospect's trust if you are to build an enduring relationship.

Put yourself in your customer's shoes and consider why they should listen to you. Do you have news they will value? Can you solve a problem they've struggled with? Have other customers like them experienced success thanks to your product or service?

Asking for their permission to begin the conversation is a crucial step in the integrated media marketing conversation. This can be straightforward, such as an ad or direct mail piece that invites them to actively *request* more information, or it can be built into the communication experience itself. Clicking on a link is implied permission. The prospect is taking action to start or continue the conversation.

The concept of "permission marketing" is an important one to consider throughout the conversations you build with prospects and customers. It demonstrates a respect for your audience and their wishes. It's a great way to start a relationship and to differentiate yourself from other marketers. Today, all marketing communications are permission-based because all consumers have a choice. You either can build that choice into your program, or they will make a choice themselves by turning the channel, deleting your e-mail, or simply tuning you out.

Good Conversationalists Are Good Listeners You've surely heard the joke about the verbose person who stops talking for a moment to ask, "Enough about me, what do you think of me?" Clearly, when it comes to an effective marketing conversation, this approach is not the same as listening to customers talk about themselves. Most marketing today is much like the self-absorbed speaker. In the typical direct "dialogue," the marketer spends most of the time selling, and then asks for a reply. The new marketing conversation is more integrated, more finely woven, and more dimensional. Your customers aren't only responding, they are driving parts of the conversation. Their role becomes an active rather than a reactive one.

This is important if you are to successfully build a connection with the prospect or customer. Disconnects occur when the two parties have different concepts of what the conversation is about. The marketer may think they are selling a thing. The customer believes the marketer is or should be fulfilling a need.

Remember, whether it makes your job easier or not, the customer controls the communication. They can walk away from your conversation at any point in time. You have to actively listen to their needs to ensure that they become, and stay engaged.

Continuing the Conversation Throughout a conversation, there are multiple points in time when one or the other participant invites their partner to continue. In body language, we convey this invitation by nodding, smiling, or looking the other speaker in the eye.

Real, and therefore satisfying, conversations are more than back-and-forth volleys of information. In a conversation, one or the other participant may take a leadership role, tell a story, or ask a question. At this point, there is an implied consent from the listener. When a prospect or customer receives communication from the marketer, they respond if it's relevant to them and give the marketer permission to continue the conversation.

As integrated media marketers, we need to identify the moments when our prospect or customer is going to respond. At these points in the conversation, we must communicate intriguing information and make offers that naturally lead them to giving us permission to continue.

Balancing Promotion and Emotion The best conversations engage feelings and intellect. Similarly, the customer relationship is a combination of promotional and emotional touchpoints. As integrated media marketers, we are responsible for orchestrating the two together.

Promotional communications include activities such as asking for information, asking for trial, asking for the sale. Emotional communications are those in which we build affinity and brand loyalty. Certain milestones and certain media lend themselves to one or the other. The total relationship comprises a blend of both.

You might choose to promote special or time-sensitive offers through direct mail, newspaper advertising, radio spots, or e-mail campaigns. Meanwhile, you can build an emotional affinity for your brand through the more experiential touchpoints of television advertising, billboards, print ads, or an entertaining or educational multimedia web experience.

Within the permission-based framework of the new marketing conversation, these two communication genres of your marketing can co-exist. In fact, they enhance each other, building brand and demand concurrently.

Question Everything A good salesperson knows that people like nothing better than to talk about themselves. As marketers, we can build this opportunity into our integrated media conversations. Include engaging response devices, customer satisfaction surveys, electronic "suggestion boxes," and other means of encouraging both feedback and proactive creative input.

Give your audience a chance to tell you what information they are looking for, as well as how they would like that information delivered. Some examples are a weekly e-mail of offers, a monthly newsletter with tips and advice, or a reminder postcard or call when a subscription renewal is due.

Conversations Are Shared Experiences We've already talked about how the combination of today's lifestyles and technology has enabled customers to drive how much marketing they actually hear and absorb. This is another strong argument for developing a conversation in which the customer takes an equal and proactive role.

A truly successful marketing conversation is one in which the customer feels as much the author of the experience as the marketer. It is this perception that will ensure the customer stays active in the conversation for the long term.

Lulls in the Conversation Sometimes a very strong friendship is marked by how comfortable the people are being quiet together. In a natural conversation there are lulls, moments of silence, when each participant reflects on what has been discussed.

Marketers must give customers a chance to direct how often they are contacted, and via what media. If you bombard the customer with messages, not only will you spend more money than necessary, but you will diminish your return. Too many promotions make customers immune to their power.

Instead, you need to time your touchpoints so that you achieve short-term response and long-term brand loyalty. As a marketer, you must continually orchestrate media, message, and relevancy.

Etiquette doyenne Emily Post wrote that an "Ideal conversation must be an exchange of thought, and not, as many of those who worry most about their shortcomings believe, an eloquent exhibition of wit or oratory." Think about your marketing programs. Are they truly an exchange of thought or are the only thoughts being exchanged yours?

Speak Their Language With customers tuning out marketing messages in ever increasing numbers, you must invest the time and money to learn what's important to them. Are you speaking their language? Your creative must resonate with your audience. Each contact must feel like a natural next step. And it must set the stage for the next touchpoint as well.

Under the Umbrella of the Marketing Conversation

Our idea of the conversation emphasizes the personal nature of integrated media marketing. This type of marketing does not promote brand awareness or make people feel good about an organization. It's only mark of success is when the prospect takes action, whether by mailing in a reply card, calling a toll-free telephone number, going to a web site, or replying to an e-mail message. This means it is an individual appeal, a conversation. Because it is a conversation, the word "you" is one of the most important words in the integrated media marketing copy.

The strategy in this conversation is always the same: get the prospect to respond. The technique to implement this strategy is nearly always the same, too:

- Step One. Get Attention
- Step Two. Describe the Benefits
- Step Three. Present the Offer
- Step Four. Ask for the Order
- Step Five. Repeat Steps Two to Four as many times as the medium allows

How you implement this technique varies from medium to medium, depending on the:

- Methods the medium allows you to use to get attention
- Number of times the medium allows Steps 2–4 to be repeated

This book gives guidelines for these two parameters for eight marketing media. It looks at examples of marketing conversations in each medium, showing how they implement the five-step technique. Before we go further, let's define our terms when speaking of the major media comprising the integrated marketing conversation.

These media divide into two broad classes: *personal media*, in which the conversation is conducted by means of an active message, and *broadcast media*, in which the conversation is conducted with an active audience.

In personal media programs, the marketer seeks the prospect. In broadcast media programs, the prospects seek the marketer. You may think that prospects seeking the marketer give the broadcast media an advantage, but in reality this advantage is more than offset by the comparatively smaller and certainly less targeted numbers of prospects in broadcast media.

It is not an either-or situation. There are strategies for combining the classes of media, as when direct mail is used to drive prospects to a web site, or a television commercial is used to get prospects to interact with a catalog.

The way integrated marketing deals with the eight basic media categories influences the message sent, and affects the type of marketing conversation you, the marketer, can hold with the consumer.

Building Your New Marketing Conversation

We've made a case for a new approach to starting and growing customer relationships across multiple media. By embracing the concept of the new marketing conversation, you'll have the ability to migrate prospects into first-time buyers, repeat customers, and—over time— into loyal advocates.

In this book, you'll learn how to develop a Creative Strategy Brief that ensures all touchpoints in your conversation achieve your objectives, deliver results, and build your brand. The template included here will give you and your team a tool to articulate the vital background information and promote the creative thinking needed to create a fruitful conversation.

Chapters on individual media describe the role for which each is ideally suited in the total integrated conversation. You'll learn how to use:

- Direct mail for one-to-one promotional offerings
- Telemarketing as a personal follow-up
- Radio to build traffic and awareness at the local level
- Television for building awareness and brand preference
- Newsletters that nurture customer relationships over time
- E-mail marketing for cost efficient updates and offers
- Web sites and advertising for research and information
- Wireless messaging and other new technologies

You'll get the tips and tools you need to put together an effective and efficient integrated media plan. Recommendations are based on determining projected return on investment (ROI), your customers' behavior and preferences, and the role each individual media selection can play in the overall conversation.

You'll also learn how marketers have implemented these principles and achieved groundbreaking results. The "Marketing Conversations in

Action" section focuses on the major marketing objectives that correspond to the customer lifecycle. These include Lead Generation, Customer Acquisition, Customer Satisfaction and Retention, Up-selling and Cross-selling additional products to customers, and Referral and Advocacy. In each chapter, we'll discuss the specific marketing objective and how the conversation approach meets the challenges generally associated with it. Then, you can review actual case studies and learn from industry leaders who have pioneered this integrated communication process.

Finally, we'll walk you through a set of tactical and operational next steps. With guidelines, templates, and worksheets, you'll have an action plan for building your own new marketing conversation.

Look Who's Talking

The good news is that customers across every industry want to be heard.

Retail customers appreciate a seamless online and offline experience. The customer browses online, downloads a coupon, shops in a brick-and-mortar store, receives a thank-you note by mail, and monthly offers for future purchases.

The Chief Information Officer takes the time to answer a long form questionnaire from a high tech supplier specifying who on his team should receive what product information, when, and via what media.

The new parent feels an emotional connection to a television spot, reads about the company's new kind of formula in a magazine, joins a chat group on a web site for answers to late-night feeding questions, and sends an e-mail registering to receive monthly coupons in the mail.

This is today's consumer. And, this is the new marketing conversation at work.

Notes

1. Figures/statistics from the Direct Marketing Association's online library.

The Role of Research and Testing in Your Marketing Conversation

Remember when you were in school? Before you could begin writing that term paper or book report you had to do some reading, take notes, gather facts, and decide what information was important enough to include and what information was not. In other words, you did your research.

Ideally, launching a marketing campaign begins much the same way: with research. Before you go full throttle into creative brainstorming, before you finalize your offer, determine your format or write a word of copy, you need to research to determine if there is an audience for the product you have in mind.

Our local middle school hosts an annual Invention Convention. It asks students to come up with an idea for a product that doesn't exist. Once their idea is approved, the research begins. Armed with questionnaires, students canvass the community to find out if there's a need or a desire for their product; what age groups the product appeals to; and how much people would be willing to pay for the new product.

Armed with this basic information, the students then determine the cost of a prototype and try to determine the cost of actual manufacture. The end result is that the students know if their product is desired and if they might be able to produce it at a cost that yields a measurable profit.

Sophisticated stuff. Yet, it's easy to see how this research effort gives the students the message either "go ahead" or "don't waste your time."

Your marketing campaign can benefit from the same approach. Research will help you determine not only if there are potential customers for your product or service but will also give you the chance to learn how you might alter or enhance the product to make it more desirable.

Research might begin with a mailer, an e-mail campaign, or a telephone survey. Your questions might not be very different from those asked by the middle school students. Whichever media you choose to conduct your research, careful thought should go into the questions. Identify what information you need and then construct your questions in such a way that makes it easy for the respondents to reply, yet still provide you with meaningful answers.

Research tools may include preprinted surveys, online survey forms, or research and survey services. Depending on your budget, your research may consist of a few dozen phone calls or hiring a research firm to conduct surveys for you. Whatever your budget, you still need to know what you want to accomplish with this research. For example, if you're certain your product is desirable you may want to know whether people will buy it in pink or blue, in wood or metal. Are you seeking greater name recognition for your brand? Are you considering a price hike? You will need to know how your client companies would respond and if they would be willing to pay more for a perceived increase in the quality of your services.

Research works hand-in-hand with testing. Common wisdom holds that research should be done before testing; research the market, then test the "big issues." Your research will actually help identify those big issues. For instance, you may begin by thinking that the marketing medium you choose is of crucial importance to your new product. After initial research, however, you may learn that the choice of medium is the least of your concerns. There's no point testing the value of e-mail versus print ads when research shows that no one wants your automatic birdseed dispenser. In this case, the big issue would be to find a representative audience who actually wants your new, improved dispenser, and then to do research to find which trigger would make your sale: Would people buy your dispenser for the convenience, the low price, its appeal to their humanitarian instincts, or because it has an uncanny ability to attract bluebirds?

Most research processes are divided into four distinct phases:

1. Preparatory research
2. Pre-testing
3. Testing
4. Post-testing

Preparatory Research

Preparatory research helps you define your target audience and the competition in the marketplace. Is there a need for your service or product? Is there an audience for it? Is that audience already well-served? Where is there room for improvement?

Compare what already exists. Which products or aspects of the product are most successful? How much are consumers currently prepared to spend? This is where you need to delve deeply into the minds of your prospective customers to anticipate how you can engage them. This is where your marketing conversation begins.

Pre-Testing

Pre-testing is where you first define what makes your product unique. Using the information you've gathered, get creative and decide how to approach consumers. At this stage, you may bring in focus groups or conduct individual interviews to provide feedback on your direction.

You might also test different forms of your message to see which one gets the greatest response. Be prepared to have some of your favorite ideas shot down. If a roundtable of twenty randomly selected people uniformly insists they don't see the value of another online investment service, it may be time to rethink your product. Perhaps your investment service needs to create a distinctive offering to set it apart from the existing choices. Your creative team might then come up with ideas for instant income calculators, or provide direct links to selected mutual fund reports, or give customers the ability to track model investments for a month. Be realistic; this is the time to first learn if your idea will translate into sales or increased brand recognition, or simply disappear into the great maw of existing product markets.

Testing

Testing itself is an ongoing process that will help you use your research to improve your initial offerings, products, and proposals. You'll be identifying areas to quantify; testing and comparing variations in the product or service and the medium or method used to reach your targeted audience; the time of day, week, month, or season that draws the biggest response; and changes in your offer, premium, or promotion.

We've mentioned using research services to send out surveys and gather basic information. At this point, it's also possible to use a Simulation Service to predict the response you may get to your campaign without actually placing an ad or buying airtime. Simulation systems work by sending a sample ad or direct mail package to a pre-chosen group of consumers who fill out questionnaires related to your product. While there are costs involved, you may ultimately save money by eliminating some factors to be tested right at the outset, depending upon the responses of the test audience. Be forewarned, though: no simulation or focus group response can *ever* replace actual in-the-market testing! People will often respond differently than they predict they will!

Copy testing can offer a chance to compare the effectiveness of your creative copy and/or the offer itself. Additionally, these results can help eliminate approaches that aren't working and reduce the number of elements to be tested in future phases. One head-to-head copy test conducted by the Milwaukee Symphony Orchestra surprised everyone by showing a four-page letter out-pulling a two-page letter. Why? Possibly because the readers of the letter, which offered a season subscription to special composer lectures in addition to regular concerts, appreciated the interesting, "gee whiz" facts about music history contained in the longer copy.

Of the three phases discussed, testing to find the best access to your targeted consumer is the most crucial, whether that means identifying the target audience or purchasing a specific list. After all, without significant audience response, your campaign will struggle to find its feet.

Post-Testing

Post-testing analysis brings the testing full-circle. In order to achieve consistent response rates in the future, it is important to clarify why consumers responded as they did. At this point, your data is measuring numbers of actual sales, requests for more information, or verifying sales leads. Be aware that even these results can be broken down into additional categories to measure the quality of each response. For instance, post-testing can help assess whether you've reached new customers or solidified your position with current customers. Post-testing will reveal the rate at which customers are converted to repeat buyers or service users. Additionally, you may be able to quantify whether your product image was enhanced by your campaign, and whether repeat or new customers are likely to buy again.

This research can establish a valuable conversation between consumer and provider. Customers who feel they are listened to, who feel they have input into the improvement or creation of a product or service are likely to value that product or service over similar products or services from less-connected providers. *They feel included in the conversation you have worked so hard to initiate.*

Secondary Research and Creativity

Much of the information that will shed light on your marketing attempts already exists through statistics and data compiled by government, private research organizations, foundations, universities, trade associations, and other entities. Statistics and demographic reports, as well as data exposing buying patterns and habits, exist at libraries and online, and are accessible through diligent searching. While it may be necessary to conduct your own secondary research to discover more about your targeted user group, it may be more effective in the long run to use a professional research organization to help you identify your most likely targets.

Just as testing is a part of research, so creativity and imagination are also an essential, yet intangible component. Countless targeted lists are already in existence; while ultimately you might not buy a list, you might contact a list sales or rental company to help identify some categories with which to conduct your research.

If, for example, you're going ahead with your automatic birdseed dispenser idea, it may be possible for you to purchase existing lists or data to learn what percentage of pet owners own birds, and on the amount of bird seed bought annually by consumers or businesses.

Secondary research that yields statistics like these may help you decide that there is a market for your automated birdseed dispenser. Logic may lead you to place test ads in birding magazines. Creativity may lead you to place test ads on bird rescue organization web sites or in the classified section of environmentalist magazines. You might contact your local Audubon Society to find statistics on how many birds are now wintering in northern climates rather than migrating south and follow up by approaching the National Audubon headquarters about acquiring their mailing and/or membership lists.

Business to Business Marketing

When marketing products or services to businesses, you're dealing with another subset of categories. Yet the same overall principles of research and testing apply: determine who is best served by your product. Contact test groups or focus groups to determine if there is a sizable need or demand for your product. This contact can be made informally or through a formally defined campaign, depending on your resources. For each organization, you'll need to find one or several contact people who make the purchase decisions. For each offer you make you will need to determine the User, the Influencer, and the Decision-maker. The benefits you present to the end-user of a telecommunications program you sell will differ from the benefits you present to the CEO of the company who may use that program. The end-user, for example, may appreciate faster access to sales leads; the decision-maker will most appreciate bottom-line benefits and over-all savings in company time and resources.

You might target professional organizations and industry publications for initial testing of your product idea. Secondary research sources may offer valuable information about competing products or services and/or help you identify areas that are under-supplied or lacking in services.

Testing offers results that measure the success of your creative efforts. Unsure which idea will get the best response? Send out three ideas to control groups and record the responses.

Testing allows you to try several variations of a program, measure responses, and then adjust the program to optimize response results. For this reason, testing is usually done on only a representative segment of an entire list, and often is split between different demographic groups.

Testing initial efforts might help identify which group responds best to the program, so you might tailor the program to a specific group or decide which group to target.

Testing efforts early will help determine the shape of your campaign; testing later will help refine and update the program.

Technically, it's possible to measure and quantify every single variable in your marketing effort. For instance, e-mails might be dissected and segmented into various elements, such as subject line, opening line, main copy, closing copy, contact information, graphic style, art or no art, color or black and white, HTML versus ASCII. On a web site, the click-through rates, the number of hits per opening page, and the percentage of responses to surveys, questionnaires, and to web site membership registration or newsletter subscriptions can be tested. Any and all media programs can test and measure general response rates, or rates varied according to format, copy, presentation, and so forth.

Another approach is to create one version and test the response to the same copy offered in different media: Internet, print, broadcast, narrowcast, or mail. Or you might test the terms of your offer, e.g., fifty percent off for a limited time only; two-for-one items; or six months free service in return for new leads.

Whether you test your entire package, the various components within the package, or even changes in the product itself, your goals should be clear: Which pulls in the greatest response? Which generates the highest response-to-buy ratio? Which generates the longest list of new prospects? Which generates more repeat visits to a store or web site? Which generates the highest percentage of contacts converting to actual sales?

You're probably beginning to see that the ability to test every aspect of a marketing effort is both an enormous opportunity and a tremendous burden. How much testing is enough? What do you test? Where do you stop? Marketing entrepreneur Hans Peter Brondmo acknowledges that you can recognize marketers as ". . . the ones who never feel they've tested and analyzed their marketing programs enough."

Faced with the potential of gathering a labyrinth of inconclusive data, the wise marketing expert employs an inspired combination of logic, intuition, creativity, and experience to decide what to test. Still, there are some general guidelines to get you started.

Many marketing professionals believe that testing the biggest differences between two direct mail packages yields more information than testing components in a single package.

Most experts agree that your marketing program should be developed in a way that lets early results be tested easily. A random sampling of various experts offers these general hints on recommended factors to test:

- Hire a testing lab, rent mailing lists, survey friends and family.
- Use controls and test the variables.
- Test the list: measure results of the same message to different lists at the same time.
- Test the offer: twenty percent discount versus ten dollars off. Extend your "Limited time only" offer.
- Test the price.
- Test the length of your message.
- Test the tone.
- Test the day and time it's sent out.
- Test varied Calls to Action: e-mail, web site, phone calls.

In short, just as you know whether the person you are having a conversation with at a party is interested in what you have to say, so too, testing will help you know how well your customer likes what you are trying to sell.

Developing a Winning Communications Strategy

In marketing, a lot of attention is paid to creative execution. Jingles work their way into our subconscious. A clever campaign is talked about at the water cooler. Super Bowl ads are front page news. But, the creative media executions that your customers see are just the tip of the iceberg. In fact, this is an excellent way to think about it.

Picture an iceberg. The part that's above the water is what your prospects and customers see, read, or hear. The part that's under the water and serves as a base or foundation for the tip that's above is actually much more massive. The underwater part includes input and information, primary and secondary research, the Creative Strategy Brief, time, talent, and lots of creative thinking. If you are looking to build a successful new marketing conversation rather than an isolated contact, pay attention to what's beneath the tip of that iceberg.

In this chapter, you'll learn the importance of developing a sound and insightful strategic foundation *before* implementing tactical communications. We've included tools to help you cover the marketing strategy basics, such as defining your objective, target audience, and value proposition. The resulting Creative Strategy Brief will ensure that all conversation touchpoints, regardless of media, converge into a persuasive and consistent overall message that moves your prospective customer from awareness to interest to engagement and, eventually, to becoming a loyal customer.

There are many different templates used for Creative Strategy Briefs. Individual ad agencies and company marketing departments usually develop their own. The format you choose to work with is less important than the information you uncover and synthesize into a succinct and actionable plan.

A well-planned and articulated Creative Strategy Brief ensures that everyone on your team is "on the same page." It allows you to build consensus before time and money are invested in creative development. By focusing on the most valuable data and insight available, you can provide the creative team with the knowledge they need to do relevant, breakthrough work. And, with this document carefully drafted in advance, marketers and other stakeholders have an objective gauge against which to judge the creative concepts and executions.

The categories of information and input that your Brief should cover include the:

- Situation Analysis
- Marketing Objectives of the campaign
- Overview of your product or service
- Value Proposition
- Profile of your audience and their needs
- Description of their current behavior—and the behavioral change you hope to affect
- Obstacles you must overcome and the corresponding bridges that the creative team can build
- Strategy, including media or format, message, and offer
- Creative Considerations
- Next Steps

Situation Analysis

Start by drafting the Situation Analysis. This important first step will help you give your entire team a common background of information from which to draw assumptions and develop ideas. In the Situation Analysis, you should describe the current market for your product or service and specifics about your company, competitive pressures, market maturity, perceptions in the marketplace, and industry trends. You should spend some time describing the competitive landscape.

Who are the other players in your market? What are they offering? And, more important, how are they communicating with their customers? It may also be helpful to chart a SWOT Analysis, highlighting your Strengths, Weaknesses, Opportunities, and Threats.

The goal here, and throughout all the sections of your Creative Strategy Brief, is to focus on the most relevant information. And remember, more is not necessarily better in this process. If you are managing a team, cull the existing resources and provide a rich, but succinct, document to work from.

Figure 3.1: Sample Situation Analysis

OVERVIEW:

Fresch & Holsum's is a new business in the Home Meal Replacement (HMR) category. It was founded in response to the following market conditions:

1. Time Poverty Epidemic: Singles, Parents and Seniors suffer from a consistent, critical shortage of time (or skills) to shop for, prepare, serve and clean-up the evening meal.
2. Healthier Food Demands: Obesity, poor nutrition, genetically modified crops–everyone is looking for a *healthy* alternative to fast food chains, expensive full-service restaurants, and especially additive-, sodium- and fat-crammed supermarket foods.
3. Drive-Thru Mania: America's new drive-thru culture is so pervasive (and profitable), alternative businesses, including pharmacies, dry cleaners, convenience stores and more, offer drive-thru and curbside service.

PRODUCT/SERVICE DESCRIPTION:

Fresch & Holsum's is a drive-thru take-out food service and walk-in "healthy mart" for customers needing a quick, convenient and inexpensive way to prepare wholesome "home-cooked" meals with minimal time spent shopping, cooking or cleaning up.

Customers order, pay and retrieve their meals in an average of two minutes. Pre-paid orders take even less time. An innovative, patented drive-thru design and Intranet-based ordering system revolutionizes the quick-service restaurant concept.

Fresch & Holsum's specializes in preparing fresh, preservative-free, take-home meals including: entrees, soups, salads, sides, desserts and baked goods. With no artificial sweeteners, colors, flavors, hydrogenated oils or synthetic preservatives. Customers have more than 50 wholesome, all-natural menu choices every day.

A revolutionary new "Virtual Commissary" strategy, leveraging co-operative supplier agreements, modern cook-chill food preparation, super-fast flash freezing techniques and space-age seal-tight packaging, allows customers to purchase and store Fresch & Holsum's products for months at a time without any loss of flavor, texture or freshness.

RESEARCH HIGHLIGHTS:

Several economic and cultural trends have contributed to the growing HMR demand:

- Increasing number of women in the workforce.
- Growing number of higher-income households.
- Americans working longer hours, with less leisure time.
- A cultural premium placed on convenience.
- Trend toward purchasing personal services.
- The top 3 reasons Home Meal Providers give for buying carryout dinners are "pressed for time" (29 %), "no energy" (27 %) and "desire home cooking" (16 %).
- A *Better Homes and Gardens* survey showed that 76 % take home prepared food for the family at least once a month.
- The heaviest users of take-home meals are DINKS (double income, no kids), but low- and middle-income families have doubled their use of restaurant take-home in the last decade.
- Currently the HMR market caters to families with an average annual household income of $50k, but by 2005, the average will be reduced to include all income levels.
- Some industry leaders have acquired quick-service meal retailers to catch some of the fallout from their own dwindling market share.

- Most supermarkets now include a deli, bakery, and a pre-pared-foods section. Also, many offer fast-food service.
- Fast-food chains are promoting healthier meals and "family-style" orders.
- Sixty percent of adults indicated they would use a drive-thru option if it was available at their favorite table service restaurant.

MARKET TRENDS:

- *Low-Carb: The Next "Big Thing."* Stores that specialize in selling low-carb foods are popping up while traditional supermarkets are clearing their shelves to accommodate this fast growing category.
- *Fast Food Dominates Daytime Takeout.* Fast food is especially dominant from 11 a.m. to 4 p.m. During the evening hours after 4 p.m., quick service and full service restaurants capture a much larger market share.
- *Eating: The Next Generation.* Young adults, who grew up on fast food, have emerged as an economic force and will make a positive impact on the HMR industry. Today's kids are already gourmands–they're no longer satisfied with macaroni and cheese or peanut butter and jelly. More "adult" food items are being created especially for kids.
- *Feeding a Changed Population.* The fastest population growth is forecast among Empty Nesters, Single Parents and Working Parents. Retail channels and foodservice providers can reach these fragmented consumer groups by addressing common consumer needs: convenience and nutrition.
- *Obesity in America.* Researchers say that if America keeps gaining weight at its current pace, virtually everyone in this country will be overweight by 2030.
- *Food Allergies Make Food Shopping an Adventure.* Retailers can play a significant role in helping families manage their diets by accommodating food allergies and offering specialty products such as gluten-free pasta.
- *Emerging Ethnic Cuisines.* Ethnic food is still an emerging business, currently worth $800 million. Retailers who provide ethnic cuisines in such a way that the consumer's time and financial commitment is minimal will own this market.

COMPETITIVE LANDSCAPE:

Fresch & Holsum's main competition will come from major supermarkets. Consumers are used to shopping at grocery stores, and 9 out of 10 these stores offer ready-to-cook entrees. However, for most supermarket retailers, food service is not a core competency, and meeting the consumer's need for convenience is an issue. Time-starved consumers don't want to wait behind moms buying groceries just to buy a ready-to-heat dinner.

Fresch & Holsum's has an advantage as a specialty store. Supermarket HMR sales only account for $8.5 billion of the total industry sales (approximately 10%), while specialty stores account for almost 50% of the total industry sales. Also, supermarkets do not provide the high-quality meals Fresch & Holsum's will, nor do they have quick service since there are usually long lines at the checkouts.

Secondary competition includes:

- Fast-food chains
- Personal chefs
- Web sites
- All natural specialty stores
- Full service restaurants
- Convenience stores & gas stations

TARGET AUDIENCE:

Fresch & Holsum's will target the five following specific market segments:

1. Families: Dual or single income, kids, no-kids, anyone who hasn't got time to breathe–or cook a healthy and delicious meal every day.
2. The "Cooking-Impaired:" Those people, who for reasons of deficient skills, cannot consistently prepare healthy and delicious meals for themselves and/or their families.
3. Healthy Eaters: Health-conscious eaters who need an alternative to grocery store, fast-food and restaurant portion sizes, fat content, sodium content and preservatives.
4. Early Adopters: Consumers who try new ideas first, when pleased, adopt the brand for many years. These consumers also serve as willing and productive advocates.

5. Caregivers: As the U.S. population ages, HMR will become a significant tool for dependent parents, rehabilitation patients, expectant mothers, foster homes and their caregivers.

Future target audiences will include:

- Commuters
- Tourists
- Home Entertainers
- Resellers
- Singles and College Students
- Government Programs, such as food stamps and "meals on wheels"

POSITIONING:

Everything Fresch & Holsum's does saves the customer time, while improving the way they eat.

- It is more than just another retail food outlet. Its focus is deliberately centered on solving customers' most pressing problems–time poverty and insufficient cooking skills.
- The foundation of Fresch & Holsum's competitive advantage is Operational Excellence. It's a new channel–in the business of distributing food, specifically natural, wholesome foods, better than anyone else.
- Fresch & Holsum's provides access to this food based upon customers' lifestyle and travel patterns. Menus are based on customers' long-term meal needs. Food is priced according to customers' budget requirements and discretionary spending habits.
- Fresch & Holsum's accomplishes all this by leveraging computer and video technology, building design, just-in-time manufacturing, outsourcing, queue / traffic management, inventory control and several other modern operational techniques.
- The company's positioning is reflected in its leading line in advertising and promotion: Fresch & Holsum's is the #1 choice for busy people who need a quick, affordable, healthy and delicious dinner "in a pinch."

Marketing Objectives of the Campaign

This is the most important part of the Creative Strategy Brief. The success of your campaign depends on whether it achieves the objectives you set or not. With this in mind, create a finite list of objectives in descending order of importance. In other words, start with the most important objective first.

As you work, consider the difference between overall program objectives and the objectives of any one project. A single touchpoint of your marketing conversation shouldn't be expected to achieve your program objective. Your overall objective may be to increase repeat sales by twenty percent but the objective of one reminder e-mail might be to achieve a five percent click-through rate.

As you're honing your objectives, try to set expectations as realistically as you can. Objectives should be relevant, obtainable, and measurable. Whenever possible, it's a good idea to create ranges until testing gives you more precise benchmarks to work with.

Some common objectives include:

- Generate XXX leads. Specify whether these come in via calls, e-mails, reply cards, web site hits, or faxes.
- Generate XXX new or repeat sales.
- Educate the audience. Try to find a way to measure this.
- Create awareness. Again, you'll want to track this.
- Test and learn.
- Establish a control.

This section should also include some discussion of your rationale for each of the objectives. You may want to match objectives to industry averages and/or explain how and why this campaign may be different. Use historical data and examples whenever possible; e.g., "Previous campaigns to the same audience generated X percent response." A summary description of economics of the business (ROI) may help illustrate what it takes to make the campaign succeed.

Overview of Your Product or Service

Describe the features and benefits of your product or service. Remember that when it comes to communicating with prospects and customers, features are much less important than benefits. A feature is what the product is or does. A benefit is what the product does for your customer.

Example:
Feature: The Lightning Laser Printer outputs color in 5 seconds.
Benefit: The Lightning Laser Printer saves you time.

In this section of the Brief, help the creative team by addressing what problem(s) the product solves. You can refer the team to existing corporate collateral or to customer input that summarizes key attributes.

Value Proposition

The value proposition is a summary statement written from the perspective of the customer. It describes the ultimate differentiators of your product or service compared to others. One good way to set this up is to complete the following sentence:

"If I choose/buy/use/try _____, I will _____."

Examples:
If I use Smilin' Brite toothpaste, I will have whiter teeth.
If I choose Cheap Talk long distance service, I'll save money.
If I buy Sure Shot golf clubs, my golf score will go up.

It's a good idea to talk to customers for a "reality check" on your product's value proposition. Sometimes customers discover additional and even better uses for a product. An extreme example is WD-40. Originally a lubricant and cleaning fluid, its users have generated more than 2,000 additional uses, from windowsill bird repellant to arthritis treatment. They've even formed an online fan club.

A Profile of Your Audience and their Needs

Describe your audience with as much detail and color commentary as you can. Remember, regardless of where you are in your conversation or what media you are using to communicate, you are selling to people, not "targets."

Start this section of the Creative Strategy Brief by listing the facts, the demographics of your best or most wanted customers. Include the basics, such as:

- Age
- Gender
- Education level
- Household or individual income
- Geography
- Industry (if it's B2B)
- Type of company
- Title and responsibilities

Then, add either researched or assumed lifestyle information:

- Values and attitudes
- Hobbies and special interests

And, because your goal is to initiate, maintain, and grow a multimedia conversation, include information about the customer's preferences, habits, and purchase behavior:

- Media usage and preference
- Typical purchase patterns

If there is more than one person involved in considering and/or purchasing your product or service, explain the situation. There may be influencers, decision-makers, coaches, and champions involved. Each will need a slightly different approach.

Example:
A marketer trying to increase applications to a university will need to engage in separate conversations with high school jun-

iors who are considering schools; high school seniors who are applying to schools; guidance counselors who are offering advice; and parents who will eventually approve and pay for the chosen school.

After you've created a profile or persona for your prospective or existing customer, describe their needs. It's particularly helpful to the creative process if you can think in terms of basic human needs, not just the specific uses of your product. Some examples are:

- Security
- Power
- Knowledge
- Health
- Money
- Pride
- Approval

The most powerful marketing messages appeal to both the rational and the emotional sides of the customer's psyche. If you can relate the benefits of your product or service to your prospect's most basic needs, you can build a very persuasive conversation.

Current and Desired Behavior

This section of the Brief comprises a description of what your prospective customer is doing today, and what you want them to do after they receive your marketing message.

How are they solving a particular problem now? Are they buying from your competition? Do they know that you offer a solution for them? How do you want their behavior to change after you've engaged them in your marketing conversation?

This section can be enhanced by putting the two perspectives—the "before" and "after"—into your customer's voice.

Example:
Before: "All breakfast bars are alike. I'll buy whichever one is on sale."

After: "Mighty Morning bars are really different. I'll have more energy if I choose Mighty Morning bars. I'm going to look for them when I shop."

Obstacles and Bridges

This section will be of particular value to your copywriter. Here, you want to describe the obstacles that may prevent your audience from noticing, reading, understanding, and taking action. Additionally, consider what inherent product or category characteristics may be barriers to their purchase decision.

As with some of the other sections in your Creative Strategy Brief, it can be helpful to write these in the first person voice of your customer.

Examples:
"I have no time."
"This will be difficult."
"This will cost too much."
"All these products are the same."
"I've never heard of your company.

Working with the list you've developed, what attributes must you promote to bridge or overcome these obstacles? Assign a response to each statement that bridges the obstacle.

Examples:

OBSTACLE	RESPONSE
"I have no time."	"This new software actually saves you time."
"This will be difficult."	"Anyone can operate the Widget Weed Eater; it's easy!"
"This will cost too much."	"For just $1.00 a day, you can help the feral chickens of Key West."
"All these products are the same."	"In independent tests, these bulbs burned twice as long."
"I've never heard of your company."	"We don't spend a lot on advertising and pass the savings on to you."

Remember, today's consumers are particularly savvy when it comes to marketing. They don't believe assertions without proof. Encourage your team to generate and use testimonials, endorsements, a list of satisfied customers, case histories, and any other relevant proof statements.

Strategy

You may want to work on this section as a team. Here, you want to determine and describe how the campaign will be constructed. What media will you use? What formats? How often will you communicate with your audience and in what sequence?

Try graphically representing the touchpoints that each prospective customer will experience. Since their input and feedback is so fundamental to the concept of the marketing conversation, build in decision-tree elements. If they respond to an e-mail, what happens next?

The offers you make to encourage response are among the most important elements in your strategy. In the marketing conversation, each offer gives the prospect or customer you're speaking to an opportunity to say "yes." These affirmations give you permission to communicate with them again. And, if your sequence is strategically sound and complements the prospect's buying pattern, these "yeses" will add up to the bigger "yes" of a purchase.

Continually testing offers is a good practice. You may want to balance informational offers, which tend to pull a lower but more qualified response, with gifts or premiums, which can yield greater numbers of less qualified leads. It's important to give the recipient of your offer multiple ways to respond. This will almost certainly increase your overall response rate. How an individual chooses to respond—by mail, by phone, or by e-mail—may provide you with valuable learning about their behavior and their media preference.

This section of the Creative Strategy Brief should also specify how many prospects will need to be touched in order to reach your response objective. To manage expectations, you may want to project three scenarios—low, average and high—based on the specific industry or your own marketing history.

Creative Considerations

One of the reasons you are investing your time and thought in the Creative Strategy Brief is to equip your creative team with everything they need to generate creative concepts for you. With that in mind, explain any graphic parameters they need to work within. Your discussion may include logo and identity specifications, existing taglines, trademarks, legal requirements, approved colors, style considerations, and other expectations.

Next Steps

This final portion of your Brief needs to be determined and agreed to by the entire team. Here, you should outline any additional research or learning that needs to happen, how the creative development should proceed, who needs to review and approve the work at each stage, and any existing or projected deadlines for production. Set expectations for the team and be sure to plan for any necessary contingencies.

Congratulations, you have just finished your Creative Strategy Brief. If time permits, put it aside for a few hours and then review it with a fresh perspective. Can it be shorter, but still contain all the relevant information? Review it from the perspective of the creative team. Review it from the perspective of the customer. Have you included everything you need to make the entire conversation and each touchpoint within it relevant and engaging?

The Creative Strategy Brief is a critical first step toward achieving your objectives. But, it is just the first step. Really effective marketing communications, like a really effective conversation, take advantage of insights and interpersonal dynamics.

Building on Your Brief

With your Brief as a foundation, you and your team can add creative and emotional power to the strategy by thinking about the prospect as an individual participant in the ongoing conversation. What matters most to the person you're talking to? What experiences—educational, entertainment, promotional or emotional—will motivate the person to stay involved in the conversation?

In drama, there's an approach known as "method acting." Performers "become" the characters they are going to portray. The idea is that if they know every detail of the character's daily life (how they take their coffee, their first teacher, their favorite color), the lines they speak will resonate with truth. You can achieve a similar truth in marketing by approaching your audience the same way.

This process encourages creative thinking about the marketing challenge, the audience, the product or service, the competition, and the offer. It is most effective when senior members of your team, especially the creative team, take part and uncover these insights firsthand.

Typical methodologies include:

- Talking to customers, prospects, sales reps, and the competition.
- Visiting the factory, the store, the lab, and the company's headquarters—anywhere that will help you absorb the company culture behind the product.
- Trying the product yourself. While you're at it, try the competition's product, too.
- Going "undercover," if necessary. Try "mystery shopping" and see if you can experience what the customer experiences. Call customer service.
- Making connections. Associate your product or offer with something that is close to the target audience's heart.
- Imagining a day in their life. If you're marketing a B2B solution to a female human resources manager, speak to her as a mother, a wife, a woman, a reader, and a golf player, as well as a professional. She is much more likely to listen.
- Reading what they read. Listening to what they listen to. Watching what they watch.
- Creating a "war room" with images that bring you closer to the visual identity of the customer.
- Finding a picture of an individual who personifies your

customer. Paste it above your desk and write to that person, one-to-one.

These methodologies fall into a handful of categories, and not every one is necessary or appropriate for every project. But the goal of this activity is to help you craft and participate in a more vital and fruitful marketing conversation.

It's worth the time and effort to get to know your prospects as individuals. No one wants to think of him or herself as someone who's a "married, white male, age 41 with a household income of $85,000." Put yourself back into that imaginary conversation. When someone is asked to describe him or herself, do they give you a demographic profile or do they talk about who they are on the inside and the things they love to do? If you can develop creative touchpoints that tap into your prospect's inner vision of who they are, you are well on your way to a winning campaign.

This is equally true in B2B marketing. Even when you are marketing a business-to-business product or solution, you must remember that there is a person on the other end. If you can relate your product or solution to their day-to-day life or to the things they truly care about, you will be much more interesting to them. And they'll want to stay in conversation with you.

If you've really listened, you know how to describe your product's benefits in a way that will matter to the person with whom you're conversing. Clever headlines may garner a smile, but they won't necessarily change behavior or generate a sale.

And remember, don't assume that you, as a marketer, know what matters to your prospect or customer. You have to ask.

Trackability and Measurability

If you've honed your Creative Strategy Brief and have been talking with your prospects and customers, you've accumulated a great deal of valuable information. How do you assess and manage all the data you've collected?

You need to track customer responses. Results should be recorded, categorized, re-categorized, and analyzed in order to help you continually revise the pitch and capitalize on those elements that elicited the greatest, most productive response.

Keep in mind that every kind of response has its value. A sale has monetary value. Increasing customer contacts and developing new leads are another valuable result. Generating repeat business from loyal customers is also valuable.

Similarly, tracking the cost-to-profit ratio of a marketing effort might help determine if the effort is worth the end result. Let's say a particular e-mail solicits two thousand hits to a company's web site, resulting in one hundred sales; a five percent conversion rate. By comparison, a print ad version of the same e-mail placed in a high-priced glossy consumer magazine elicits a higher seven percent conversion rate. Yet, when you compare the high cost of buying the ad space versus the relatively low cost of the e-mail campaign, the end result shows the e-mail campaign yields higher profits.

Tracking cost versus response also enables you to calculate return on investment (ROI). Storing this information in a database takes the process a step further. Besides knowing the relative profit or return on investment of a particular marketing effort, the same data can be interpreted to yield valuable demographic information, e.g., showing buying patterns according to region or gender, or tracking customers in terms of credit ratings and payment history.

Still, it's important to remember that all the effort put into gathering, recording, and analyzing and categorizing responses is directed to one purpose: creating profitable customers as opposed to one-time sales. As direct marketing legend Martin Baier asserts: "It's about creating new customers and cultivating current customers. Who are they? Where are they? How are they created? What is their lifetime value?"

Establishing a winning communication strategy enables you to establish relationships with customers. It's a personal dynamic, much closer to our idea of a conversation than a sales pitch. Marketing works by first initiating contact with potential customers. Contact leads to opportunities to initiate the marketing conversation. Continuing contact builds the relationship, or dialogue, to keep customers coming back for more products and services.

The Media of the Conversation

Direct Mail

A side from a direct sales call, direct mail is perhaps the oldest, most familiar form of a personal selling and marketing medium.

Types of Direct Mail

Certainly everyone in the United States has received a piece of direct mail marketing, whether a simple postcard announcement of a product or service, a fundraising package with name-and address labels enclosed, or a complex magazine-sweepstakes mailer that includes a letter, magazine stamps, a variety of reply cards, special offers within the offer, prize stamps, return envelopes, and so on.

Direct mail can be directed toward house lists of existing or lapsed customers or sent out as cold prospecting acquisition efforts.

The physical forms of direct mail include:

- Standard envelope formats
- Self-mailers
- Billboard mailers
- 3-D product mailers
- Catalogs
- Magalogs
- Advertorials
- CD or video mailers
- Single, double, and triple postcards
- Card or coupon packs

Most of these forms are self-explanatory. Self-mailers and billboard mailings are simplified versions of standard envelope packages, while double and triple postcards are more elaborate variations of single postcards. Postcards, card packs, or coupon packs vary from simple sale announcements to offers for free or discounted products and services.

Three-D product mailers may be boxes or envelopes containing samples of actual products and are often used for high-dollar product lead-generation efforts in business-to-business marketing. Catalogs contain product illustrations and text, usually written in an inverted pyramid style with most important copy information on top. They can be utilitarian or high-concept productions. Many catalogers have discovered that including extra information—recipes, decorating tips, author interviews, and so forth—ensure that the catalog becomes a "keeper" and has extra life in the hands of the recipient.

Magalogs are most often specific-interest catalogs disguised as magazines, and designed to generate interest in products or services, such as travel clubs, auto insurance clubs, magazines, or drug companies. These combine informative editorial content with a standard direct mail letter and offer postcard and can often run eight to twelve or more pages in length.

Advertorials are advertisements designed to resemble editorial material in magazines or newspapers. Just as product placement of cereals, candy bars, or cars in popular movies can build brand awareness, placing editorial content in a publication is another way to sell. It is key for any marketer using advertorials to include an 800 number, URL, mail address, or reply coupon to offer a response mechanism and fully engage in the new marketing conversation.

Compact discs (CDs) or video mailers, the latest additions to personal marketing methods, may contain instructional information detailing how to use a product; enticing "ads" complete with pitches and testimonials for products or services; or even entertainment, such as excerpts of video games or elaborate musical productions. Nintendo, AT&T, AOL, and many other companies have used CD mailings in their marketing campaigns.

Today, everyone from wood stove manufacturers to DisneyWorld sends out CDs, DVDs, or videotapes to provide information, and to give the consumer the experience of using the product or visiting the site, making the product even more personal and more desirable.

The advantage of *any* type of personal mailer is that 1) it is directed exclusively to the recipient, and 2) the consumer can keep it and refer to it again, browsing through favorite catalogs or viewing informational videotapes. And unlike electronic marketing (Internet, television, and radio), the direct mail promotion is thrust directly into the prospect/customer's hands. While consumers may view radio, television, and print ads casually and unconsciously, personal mailers require at least some active participation by the consumer. Each piece must be handled as it is taken from the mail box or post office box.

Catalogs, magalogs, advertorials, CDs, and videos can create a substantial desire for goods about which the consumer was unaware before seeing the pictures or reading the copy. In this way, personal mailers work to both fill a need and to create a need.

One disadvantage of personal mailers is that they can be easily discarded. Unlike radio, television, or print ads that are repeated over and over again, personal mailers easily run the risk of being discarded into File #13, i.e., the trash can.

Direct mail also includes the category of space advertisements in magazines and newspapers. Print publications can be targeted specifically by location or special interest, and easily used by advertisers to reach specific audiences. Magazines are most often tailored to specific interests, such as X-treme sports, Victorian houses, or vegetarian cooking. They can offer a particular point of view on current events, represent the members of service or religious organizations, or reflect the lifestyles of particular cities or regions.

Since newspapers are marketed in broad to narrow markets—national, regional, or local—their advertisements can be easily targeted and directed not only toward special interest groups, but to special interest groups within specific cities, towns, or neighborhoods.

The Direct Mail Conversation

There are those who consider direct mail the foundation of all marketing from which all marketers can learn lessons to apply to marketing in other media. Why? Direct mail is targeted, personal, and interactive. It has been used and thoroughly tested for years. We've learned what works, and while new breakthroughs do occur, some of the best advice we can give any marketer is to follow some of the tried-and-true principles of direct mail advertising. What are these principles?

Certainly the primary guiding principle of direct mail is that it is a one-to-one, personal communication. Your direct mail package should usually include a letter to take advantage of this personal touch, and that letter should sound as though it has been written by one human being to another. Even if you are sending a self-mailer or catalog, you can consider putting a short letter with salutation and signature on one panel. You'll often find such a letter on the upper left hand corner of the inside cover of a catalog or brochure, for example, a letter from the company president introducing the company and its product or mission.

Another principle of successful direct mail is that your creative should be developed to convince and please the customer, not to win awards. An important question to ask is: "Does this make sense to the customer?" Your art department may suggest tiny white drop-out type on a turquoise background, but if your customer can't read that type, you've blown your chance to start a conversation and make a sale.

Usually, body copy and letter copy in a direct mail piece will be set in serif type because it's easiest to read in a print format.

A good formula to remember when creating direct mail is A-I-D-A, which stands for:

- Attention
- Interest
- Desire
- Action

One of the first places you grab your prospect's attention is on the outer envelope or front panel of a self-mailer. The copy that's written there is called the teaser copy. Your reader will usually devote no more than a second or two to looking at your outer envelope, so the teaser copy is a key element in whether a direct mail package gets opened. There are various ways to write effective teasers:

1. Start a story
2. Promise a benefit
3. Offer a discount
4. Provoke curiosity
5. Call for action
6. Announce news
7. Invoke urgency

Teenagers and young adults learn quickly which lines work well and which bomb as they try to maneuver the dating scene. What's a good opener? In direct mail, you can test the success of various openers by changing the teaser copy on the outer envelope. Don't forget that the back of the envelope is a good place to highlight your sales message, too.

Some copywriters suggest that you start the letter with the same words you use on the outer envelope, assuming that if the teaser copy worked to get them inside the package; it will work again to get them into the letter.

In general, you'll want to use short paragraphs—no more than three or four lines, and incorporate bulleted lists, sentence fragments, underlining, second color, and handwriting, as appropriate. These are all ways to highlight certain elements, or as expert copywriter and catalog consultant Pat Friesen calls them, hot spots, of your letter. Your reader won't read your prose word for word, but you can still make your sale if you make it easy for him or her to understand your message in what are basically sound bites. The Johnson box (the copy that appears above the salutation) and the postscript are both hot spots on a letter—places where a reader will go to read the most important part of your message.

There's no rule as to the length of your letter other than it should be long enough to tell your tale and make your sale. Many financial services and telecommunications companies successfully use one-page letters, sometimes with a response form attached. Some stock market newsletters use eighteen page letters in their direct mail packages! Generally, you can write longer copy if you are mailing to readers and/or people who are interested in what you have to say.

It's good to include "gee whiz" facts in your copy, just as you sprinkle your spoken conversation with interesting tidbits at a cocktail party. Another good trick is to use "bucket brigade" words to help move the flow of your copy from paragraph to paragraph. Sample "bucket brigade" words are "that's why," "here's how," and "now."

Unlike spoken conversation, the copy in a direct mail package is subject to revision. A good copywriter will edit ruthlessly—taking out every unnecessary word or stumbling block. He or she will make sure copy at the end of a page doesn't end with a period—a sure conversation stopper. Instead, it's better to break mid-sentence, and even better to make that mid-sentence break a cliff-hanger so your reader just *has* to turn the page to see what comes next.

The conversation between copywriter and reader can continue on a brochure. Here, the conversation can get more detailed. Listings of product features or measurements can be included. There can be photographs of the product in use or testimonials from happy customers. If you're offering something FREE or at SPECIAL SAVINGS, emphasize that. Don't hide your light under a bushel.

Other items inside the package can include a buck slip or insert highlighting a limited quantity or special sale. This piece should look like it's been stuck into the package just at the last minute—like a sudden verbal interruption.

There may also be a component called a lift letter—a secondary letter signed by someone other than the signer of the main letter. The lift letter is an opportunity to augment your sales message by featuring a new benefit or further reassuring the prospect. The teaser copy on the outside panel of a lift letter may say something like "Open only if you've decided not to accept this offer . . ."

Every piece inside a direct mail package should direct the reader to the response form. After the outer envelope—which is your first, best chance to make your sale—this is the most important part of the package. Make sure your response form looks like a response form. Give it a title: SAVINGS CERTIFICATE or MEMBERSHIP ENROLLMENT FORM or RISK-FREE OFFER. Make it easy to understand and complete. Offer several payment options and return options. Restate any money-back guarantee. Feature any premium or discount savings or deadline. State concisely your most important benefit, i.e. your answer to the reader's question of "What's in it for me?" Benefits can often be written to begin with the most important word in all direct marketing copy: you. "You'll discover . . . learn . . . grow . . . enjoy. . . ."

The key ending to any conversation in direct mail is the call to action. That's why it's imperative you send your reader to your response form from every package component and make it easy for him or her to respond to your initial approach, whether they do so by fax, mail, phone, or your web site.

Good conversationalists—and good direct mail copywriters—know that if they want a response they need to be clear about what response they want to elicit. They need to know intuitively when their copy is boring the reader, how to grab them from that first opening line of the letter and not let go. An old time salesman sitting on a couch across from a housewife could tell when she was getting bored, when she began looking at her watch or toward the kitchen. He'd change his tactic then—maybe dump the contents of an ashtray on the floor to get her attention and demonstrate his product. Today, a copywriter doesn't have the advantage of seeing the facial reactions or gestures of their prospect. But even looking at the computer screen, the copywriter must place himself or herself in the shoes of that housewife, IT person, or CEO and know what words to use to get attention, hold attention, and close the deal.

The Art of the Questionnaire

by Alan Rosenspan

You're about to throw away a direct mail package, and you suddenly realize, "Wait a minute—there's a real dollar bill stuck in here!" So you continue reading and find out it's a questionnaire and the company sending it is offering you a small reward to "thank you in advance" for filling it out.

Uh, oh . . . what do you do now?

Do you answer all the questions honestly and completely, because after all, they *paid* for your opinion? Do you answer in the nicest possible way—because, after all, they were nice enough to trust you with the cash up front? Or do you quietly pocket the bill, delight in the fact that you just got something for nothing, and toss away the questionnaire?

Let's talk about questionnaires and what makes them such a powerful direct marketing tool.

Do questionnaires really work?
Do they ever!

What's an average response to one of your direct mail packages? A typical questionnaire or survey gets response rates as high as 10–20%. And if you're mailing to customers, and not prospects, you can do even better. We did a questionnaire for Lucent Technologies that generated a 28% response. We did one for Datawatch that generated over 4,000 responses.

I'll let you in on a secret—questionnaires and surveys work so well, they can be used to boost response—even when you *don't care* about the answers. We included a short questionnaire in a direct mail package we did for AT&T. I have to confess we weren't just interested in their opinions—we wanted to get them to come back to AT&T. Response jumped over 20%. Where did we put the questionnaire? Right on top of the reply card—and for a very good reason. To answer the questions, a prospect requires a pen or pencil. And isn't that *exactly* what they'll need to fill out their reply card?

11 Ways to Improve Response to Your Next Questionnaire

1. Make the questionnaire the "hero" of the package, not just another element.
2. Fewer questions are better—7–11 are ideal. For some reason, odd numbers seem to work better than even numbers.
3. Include a letter to "Thank you in advance." Tell them why their answers are important. Tell them what they get.
4. Have the letter come from someone important at your company.
5. Give them an offer. It could be entry into a sweepstakes, a premium, or even the fact that you will share the results with them. So they'll know what other people, just like them, are thinking.
6. Include a "Thank you" message on the actual questionnaire.
7. Include the offer on the actual questionnaire. Use a photograph of it, if possible.
8. Make the questions very simple, "Yes" and "No" works best. Asking people to estimate their projected sales revenue for 2005 might be too difficult—and give them a reason to toss it.
9. Make sure you include a space for comments or suggestions. No matter how smart you are, you'll never be able to anticipate every issue. Give them room to write in what they want.
10. If appropriate, reassure them that their answers will be kept confidential and will not be used for solicitation (unless they will be, of course.)
11. Give people a way to respond online.

So you've sent out a questionnaire—and you've garnered a terrific response. And you're sitting with a pile of thousands of completed surveys. What should you do with them now? If you're like most companies, the only thing you do is tabulate the results, and put them in a report for future generations. Unfortunately, that's the *worst* thing to do.

You need to (1) let people know you received their answers and thank them; (2) respond to their comments or suggestions; and (3) try to fix any problems they've reported. So when you're considering a questionnaire, consider actually using the suggestions and comments, and providing feedback to the respondents.

In summary, questionnaires can accomplish a number of important functions in a direct marketing campaign.

They can help you identify issues that are important to your prospects; prioritize leads; ensure customer satisfaction; promote interaction; and build better relationships. Most importantly, they can generate a *mountain* of leads.

So should you do a questionnaire? *Do you even have to ask?*

When he isn't writing copy, Alan Rosenspan writes articles and speeches. He's posted about 35 of them on his web site at www.alanrosenspan.com, Reprinted with permission of Alan Rosenspan.

Telemarketing

One of the most obvious examples of a marketer-to-customer or marketer-to-prospect conversation is a telemarketing call, usually, though not always, conducted by two human voices. Whether delivered live or via recording, telephone solicitations have become a constant of our lives. If the sales pitch is offered by a human being, it can be the most personal kind of marketing effort. For example, telemarketing continues to be especially effective in generating donations to local or national charities. The DialAmerica program has long been a partner of both the Special Olympics and Mothers Against Drunk Driving, offering discounted magazine subscriptions with an automatic donation (Special Olympics) or soliciting straight donations (MADD).

In these cases, the "personal touch" may be more effective coming by phone, whereas messages for credit card protection or long distance dialing plans might not be greeted as enthusiastically.

The Promise and the Problem

Here, both the potential and pitfall of marketing conversations can be readily seen. Telemarketing, a $540 billion industry consisting almost entirely of ethical, hard-working people, gets little respect outside of marketing circles. Public opinion on telemarketing is illustrated by the lively market in devices designed to prevent it. At least one of these purports to intercept a telemarketing call, then return a signal on the telephone line that removes the user's record from the telemarketer's computer. It may not be legal or even possible to make an unauthorized change in a caller's database. However, it's clear that telemarketing is one of the few industries that inspire enough public hostility to have generated an open trade in products designed to sabotage it.

The particular application that causes this otherwise dynamic and intensely personal marketing medium to be viewed negatively is technically called outbound business-to-consumer customer-acquisition telemarketing. It is more commonly thought of as the unwanted-call-during-dinner application. If you go to the web's most popular search engine and enter the word "telemarketing," seventy percent of the links on the first results page point to sites that fight against it, including the U.S. Federal Trade Commission. In June 2003, the Federal Trade Commission (FTC) created a national "Do Not Call List." As of the publication of this book, more than fifty million people have registered. The web site for the list, *http://www.donotcall.gov,* provides information for marketers, as well as consumers.

It is probably the general public's attitude that causes many list owners to instruct brokers not to release their lists for telemarketing.[1]

Despite the negative associations, telemarketing is nevertheless a powerful medium. You should consider telemarketing applications, including outbound cold-calling, as part of your marketing conversation, with careful attention not to schedule calls at dinnertime in the target time-zone.

Putting Telemarketing to Work

Fortunately, it is possible to conduct a telemarketing campaign in a way that does not antagonize its audience. The speed of response and the flexibility of the medium (it may be the only medium in which you can change your copy once the campaign has rolled out) mean that a well-planned and well-executed telemarketing program is generally successful.

Finally, if you have a base of satisfied customers, they probably want to hear from you. Let's review the basics of this powerful and personal marketing medium.

Telemarketing falls into two broad application areas: inbound and outbound. Each of these can be applied to both business-to-consumer

and business-to-business. Outbound telemarketing, whether business-to-consumer or business-to-business, can be subdivided further
into lead generation, customer acquisition, and customer reactivation
or renewal.

Technology, Staff, and List: Telemarketing in the Real World

While this chapter is not a comprehensive study of this medium, it is
important to see how telemarketing works in the real world before we
start writing any scripts.

Recently, the cost of a completed outbound telemarketing call has declined significantly. Predictive dialing, automated call distribution, voice
recognition, and targeted databases are all technologies that help a telemarketing organization connect with prospects reliably and inexpen-
sively. In fact, if you don't have the technology at your disposal, you
probably won't be able to implement telemarketing cost-effectively.
Without the technology, the cost of incomplete calls, high refusal rates,
or both, is prohibitive, particularly for outbound telemarketing. Inbound
telemarketing has a technology of its own and, although its call completion rate is limited only by the number of lines and operators you maintain, it also can be expensive if you don't automate it properly.

Copywriting does not play as large a role in telemarketing as it does in
any of the other media. With mail, print, the Internet, and, to a certain
extent, video, the prospect generally interacts directly with your words.
But with telemarketing, the prospect interacts with a person using your
words. In direct mail, for example, with outstanding copy and a great
offer, you can sometimes get a certain number of readers to overlook a
poor presentation, i.e., the design or printing. But the best copy and
greatest offer in the world can do almost nothing to overcome a poor
presentation in telemarketing because the prospects will not stay on the
line long enough to hear it. Because of telemarketing's reputation, most
people who own telephones are not anxious to hear a pitch, and they are
increasingly sophisticated at detecting and avoiding them.

The key to presentation is skilled callers. If your telemarketing caller doesn't have the skill to put prospects at ease; to listen for real rather than nominal objections; to ask for the order at the right moment; to upsell receptive prospects; and to downsell when necessary, the best script in the world has very little chance of success.

Along with technology and caller skill, the third major success factor in telemarketing is list selection. List selection is a major success factor in all marketing media, of course, but with mail and e-mail, it is primarily important as the mechanism for getting your offer in front of the right people. You can personalize direct mail and you should. But what is a response booster in direct marketing is a prerequisite in telemarketing. You must know whom you're calling before you speak to the person.

In addition to having a high-quality list, you should also have one that is segmented by various criteria. The reason for this is that telemarketing is a real-time medium. If, in a given campaign, you get a high refusal rate among a certain kind of prospect early in the cycle, you can remove similar prospects from the list and reduce costs for the rest of the cycle. Let's illustrate with an example:

> Say you are doing customer acquisition for a conservation organization based on a campaign called "Making Peace with Nature." Among the many lists with which you've had good results in the past is a hunting magazine, because hunters tend to be conservationists. So, you base your campaign on a consolidated list that includes subscribers from that hunting magazine. But early in the campaign, you notice certain prospects are not only cool to the pitch of "Making Peace with Nature," they are actively hostile. A quick analysis shows you that the readers of the hunting magazine are indeed conservationists, but they see the slogan "Making Peace with Nature" as an attack on hunting.
>
> If your list is segmented, you can withdraw the hunting magazine subscribers from the campaign. If, on the other hand, you don't know who among your prospects are subscribers or you have no way of removing them, you will be forced to continue calling them. Calling alienated prospects does more than simply raise your costs; it generates hostility to your cause in a significant group of people.

Because the technology and training for telemarketing are so specialized, there are a number of third-party vendors available to supply it.
Agencies like AB&C Group or DialAmerica Marketing can provide an
organization with a fully staffed facility for a telemarketing program. In
fact, telemarketing is often conducted on a pay-for-performance or per-
inquiry basis, which minimizes up-front costs. Whether you contract
with an agency or manage it in-house, make certain you will be working with a good list that can be segmented, reliable call center technology, and well trained callers.

A Template for the Telemarketing Conversation

There are two basic approaches to developing copy for telemarketing:
call guide or script. A call guide consists of suggested wording for certain segments of the call, such as the introduction, and substantial lists
of product features and benefits that can be woven into conversation.
Call guides are most often used with in-house telemarketers selling
small numbers of products that they know well. They are probably best
suited to inbound sales that are not tied to a particular campaign, since
in that case, the telemarketer needs to have maximum flexibility for
dealing with a wide variety of call types.

The advantage of a call guide is that it can make the call more spontaneous and interactive. It has several disadvantages, the chief one being
that it gives you less control over the pitch. The call guide usually makes
each call take longer. Without a script showing when to ask for the order,
most people, no matter how well trained, will delay doing so, resulting in
longer calls, which mean higher costs. Now we'll look at a script.

To review, the basic marketing strategy is in five steps:

Step 1. Get Attention
Step 2. Describe the Benefits
Step 3. Present the Offer
Step 4. Ask for the Order
Step 5. Repeat Steps Two to Four as many times as the
medium allows.

Telemarketing requires an extra step before Step One because it utilizes human contact, and must observe human courtesies. It requires that most basic of social interactions, the introduction, and the introduction takes place before you try to get attention. For reasons we discuss, it combines the steps of describing benefits and presenting the offer. Here, then, is the telemarketing strategy for your script:

Step 1. Introduction
Step 2. Get Attention
Step 3. Describe the Benefits and Present the Offer
Step 4. Ask for the Order
Step 5. Repeat Steps Three and Four.

Step One: Introduction Even before the introduction, telemarketing requires that you locate the prospect. So, there is even a brief step before the introduction, a connection request. Since the invention of the telephone, no one has really improved on this as a line to request connection:

"Hello. May I please speak to _____?"

Note that this line does not use "Mr." or "Ms." It is unsafe to use that designation unless you are sure of the prospect's gender. Modern names increasingly hide gender, and you can't always rely on the data provided in your list. Until you actually speak to the prospect and get some indication of the person's gender, it is best not to assume. It also is best not to ask for the prospect by first name. Using the first name alone makes it sound like you are a friend or acquaintance. This may get a higher call completion rate, but it also creates a deceptive tone that can backfire. So, ask for the prospect by both first and last name, "Hello. May I please speak to Ashley Wilkes?"

After you have requested the connection, you can state the introduction, and you may have to do it more than once. The person answering the phone, for example, may ask you for identification before locating the prospect. You respond with the introduction:

"My name is _____ I'm calling for *Nature's Peace* magazine."

When you give your name, you use both first and last name. In this case, if you try to use only your first name, you run risk of sounding deceptive or familiar, both of which are likely to be unsuccessful. Once connected with the prospect, restate the introduction:

"Hello. My name is _____. I'm calling for *Nature's Peace* Magazine."

If appropriate, you can insert, "Thanks for taking my call."

It can be an effective strategy to finish the introduction with a question that elicits a positive response from the prospect. Traditionally, that question is "How are you today?" These days, most people don't believe the caller really cares how they are and consider the question insincere. The classic "Have I caught you at a good time?" can be dangerous because it gives the prospect an excuse to end the call.

What you want is a question that gets a positive response in order to begin the conversation agreeably. Avoid questions about politics, current events, and sports, as people tend to have strong opinions about these subjects that you can't predict.

This would seem to leave little besides the weather, but you should avoid that unless you know the weather in the prospect's area, which will change from day to day and perhaps more often than that. DialAmerica suggests "Can you hear me?" It is a particularly good question because nearly all prospects will respond positively, and they can do so without committing themselves to anything.

Step Two: Get Attention It's important to remember that outbound telemarketing calls to consumers are subject to federal regulations, which require the caller "to disclose promptly and in a clear and conspicuous manner" the identity of the seller; that the purpose of the call is to sell goods or services; and the nature of the goods or services. Identifying yourself in the Introduction covers part of this. The best way to cover the rest is to use it to *Get Attention*. How do you do that? Announce the premium:

"I'm calling, Mr. or Ms. Prospect, to tell you we'd like to send you a gorgeous, full-color wildlife calendar as a gift with your paid subscription to *Nature's Peace* magazine."

This assumes, of course, that there is a premium. A quality premium is your best chance of getting the prospect's attention. It also lets you tell the prospect this call is about what you can do for her at the same time as you make your "clear and conspicuous" statement that you are calling to sell her something. Combining the purpose of the call, selling with the offer of a premium, is more than a way to get attention; it also can increase the cost-effectiveness of the telemarketing itself. If the premium is well-chosen, it helps to qualify the prospect. Most people will recognize at this point that it is a sales call, and those with no interest will try to terminate the call. Getting an early end to a call to an unqualified prospect lowers your cost. Those who are interested in the premium pre-qualify themselves and will be more receptive to the pitch.

Step Three: Describe the Benefits and Present the Offer With telemarketing, Steps Two and Three must be compressed so that the benefits are presented and the offer is made at the same time. Before we discuss this in more detail, let's have a look at the importance of a good offer.

Most direct marketers assume forty percent of a marketing program's success comes from having the right audience; twenty percent from having the right message; and forty percent from having the right offer. The offer is always important because it is what the prospect decides on. With telemarketing, unlike the other media, there are no color brochures or other collateral materials to support the pitch. Few prospects are going to sit still while the telemarketer tries to create a word picture. The offer must be compelling, and it must be presented early in the call. You can't put the offer too far ahead of the benefits, however, so the best strategy is to combine both in one step.

The most difficult part about writing this section of the script is to keep the offer brief. As with any offer presentation, you want to make certain the prospect hears the benefits. In other media, extensive lists of benefits will probably support the sale. In telemarketing, a long list of benefits will lose more sales than it will gain. Limit yourself to one or two benefits.

Procedurally, the best way to deal with this step is to consult the exhaustive list of benefits you compiled for your marketing conversation and select the one or two most attuned to the needs of your audience. Don't discard the others. You will need them for Step Five. Select your strongest benefits and make the offer:

> "As part of this promotion, Mr. or Ms. Prospect, you can receive a full year of the world's most beautiful nature magazine for the low price of $18.95—that's 75% off the cover price. If you aren't inspired by the joys of the natural world within your first two issues of *Nature's Peace* magazine, just write 'cancel' on the invoice, you'll owe us nothing, and you can keep your free calendar."

The quality of the offer is critically important in telemarketing, and because there is such widespread mistrust of the medium, the best offer will always include some way to eliminate the prospect's risk, such as a money-back guarantee, a thirty-day approval, or a no-questions-asked refund or cancellation.

Step Four: Ask for the Order It has been a fairly short conversation so far, but if you presented the offer and the benefit, it's time to ask for the order. Remind the prospect of the premium, the benefits, and the guarantee. Then ask:

> "This is the best offer we've ever made to new subscribers, Mr. or Ms. Prospect. I can send your free wildlife calendar and activate your risk-free one-year subscription to *Nature's Peace* magazine right now. OK?"

Notice how the offer takes an affirmative stance and simply asks the prospect for an approval.

Step Five: Repeat Steps Three and Four Step Five is critical in telemarketing because the overwhelming majority of prospects will say no to the first offer. For the handful that says yes, the call can be completed. For those who say anything else, your script has to be ready to handle the refusal. There is a necessary transition, however. Before proceeding to Step Five, you must agree with the prospect:

> "Yes, Mr. or Ms. Prospect, we all feel like we are receiving too many magazines these days."

The importance of agreeing with the prospect is fundamental. When you disagree with the prospect's objection, you give him or her something to defend. Not all telemarketers believe it is important to repeat the prospect's objection. Some prefer to agree and change the subject. If you do repeat the objection, it can deepen trust because it signals the prospect you are listening. You may want to test both strategies with your audience. If you decide to repeat the objection, you probably cannot script it, but you can train your callers to do it.

As soon as you've agreed with the prospect, proceed to Step Five:

> "That's why we're offering to send you *Nature's Peace* without charge. If it doesn't brighten your life within two issues, just write 'cancel' on the invoice. You can keep the gorgeous wildlife calendar in any case. OK?"

If the prospect objects again, the next repetition should use your next strongest benefit:

> "Yes, Mr. or Ms. Prospect, we all have so little time these days. That's why *Nature's Peace* wants to help you decompress from your hectic schedule with beautiful nature photos every month. Every page of every issue includes the most exquisite color photographs of natural scenes from the world's foremost wildlife photographers, the same ones who made the photos for our gorgeous wildlife calendar. If, for any reason whatsoever,

you're not 100% satisfied with your subscription to *Nature's Peace* within the first two issues, just write 'cancel' on the invoice. The calendar is yours to keep. OK?"

Script three to four repetitions, moving down your benefits list until you have exhausted your strongest ones.

A Sample Script Here's how the template might look for a cold call:

1. Introduction	**Caller:** Hello. My name is _____. I'm calling for *Nature's Peace* magazine. Thanks for taking my call. Can you hear me?
	Prospect: Yes
2. Get Attention	**Caller:** I'm calling, Mr. or Ms. Prospect, to tell you we'd like to send you a gorgeous, full-color wildlife calendar as a gift to go with your paid subscription to *Nature's Peace* magazine.
3. Benefits & Offer	**Caller:** As part of this promotion, Mr. or Ms. Prospect, you can receive a full year of the world's most beautiful nature magazine for the low price of $18.95—that's 75% off the cover price. If you aren't inspired by the joys of the natural world within your first two issues of *Nature's Peace* magazine, just write 'cancel' on the invoice, you'll owe us nothing, and you can keep your free calendar. This is the best offer we've ever made to new subscribers, Mr. or Ms. Prospect.
4. Ask for Order	**Caller:** I can send your free wildlife calendar and activate your risk-free one-year subscription to *Nature's Peace* magazine right now. OK?
	Prospect: No. I already receive too many magazines.

5. Repeat 3–4   **Caller:** Yes, Mr. or Ms. Prospect, we all feel like we are receiving too many magazines these days. That's why we're offering to send you *Nature's Peace* without charge. If it doesn't brighten your life within two issues, just write "cancel" on the invoice. You can keep the gorgeous wildlife calendar in any case. OK?

Notice that this sample script is for cold calls. If you're doing customer renewal or reactivation, you have the power of being able to address your prospect as "a customer" or, better yet, "one of our best customers." Telemarketing is an extremely powerful medium for customer renewal or reactivation.

A Customer Renewal Strategy Here's how the template might look for a renewal:

1. Introduction   **Caller:** Hello. My name is _____. I'm calling about your subscription to *Nature's Peace* magazine. Thanks for taking my call. Can you hear me?
Prospect: Yes.

2. Get Attention   **Caller:** We're calling selected subscribers, Mr. or Ms. Prospect, to tell you we'd like to send you a gorgeous, full-color wildlife calendar as a gift for renewing your subscription to *Nature's Peace* magazine.

3. Benefits & Offer   **Caller:** As part of this special renewal program, Mr. or Ms. Prospect, your renewal is only $18.95—that's 75% off the cover price. As always, if you aren't completely satisfied with your subscription to *Nature's Peace* magazine, you can cancel at any time for a full refund on unsent issues. The full-color wildlife calendar is yours to keep no matter what.

4. Ask for Order	**Caller:** This is the best renewal offer we've ever made, Mr. or Ms. Prospect. I can send your free wildlife calendar and activate your risk-free subscription renewal right now. OK? **Prospect:** No. I'm trying to cut back on magazines.
5. Repeat 3–4	**Caller:** Yes, Mr. or Ms. Prospect, we all feel like we are receiving too many magazines these days. That's why we give you a satisfaction guarantee with your renewal. If *Nature's Peace* doesn't continue to brighten your life the way it has for the past year, just cancel, and we'll refund the unexpired portion of your subscription, no questions asked. You can keep the gorgeous wildlife calendar in any case. OK?

Note that the introduction step of this call mentions the prospect's history with the product ("I'm calling about your subscription to *Nature's Peace* magazine."). In this call, you are capitalizing on your existing or previous relationship with the prospect. You must find a low-key way to remind the prospect of that relationship. And in Step Five, the word "continue" is used specifically to reinforce that relationship. Otherwise, it is basically the same script as the one for a new customer, with the details changed to fit a renewing customer.

The Marketing Conversation in a Business-to-Business Environment

So far, we have discussed the business-to-consumer application, but telemarketing can do particularly well for business-to-business opportunities. Business people expect to receive sales calls. This is probably the reason why business-to-business telemarketing calls are not subject to the same local and national regulations as business-to-consumer calls.

Businesses have organized themselves to deal with telephone sales calls. Thirty years ago, almost anyone who might be in a position to approve a purchase had other people to take and screen calls. Today, the screening is largely done by voicemail.

To the telemarketer, it may look like voicemail systems and human call screeners are designed to prevent callers from reaching callees. But, in fact, most business professionals consider it part of their job to listen to sales pitches, and generally there is a way to get through.

The absolute best way to get through to a business decision-maker with a telemarketing call is to be the person who can solve that decision-maker's problem. How can you let the prospect know if you can solve her problem if you can't get through to her? When leaving a message, describe your premium:

> "We're sending our just-published *Guide to High-Performance Server Software* to a selected group of companies, and I wanted to know if you are the person who should receive it."

This approach only works if the premium is related to your product, and in a business-to-business market your premium ought to be related to your product. Mugs, tee shirts, pens, and the like can be useful to hand out at trade shows. If you're trying to make a sale, your marketing conversation begins with a premium that both helps the prospect in his job and moves his thinking in the direction of your product. A mug doesn't do that. This illustrates another aspect of business-to-business telemarketing: it is nearly always directed at lead generation. In business-to-consumer, the telemarketers are the salespeople, but in business-to-business, telemarketers fill the role of traditional marketers: preparing and qualifying the prospects so professional sales people can deal with them. A premium that promises to put the prospect on the path of solving her major business problem is the best way to start that process. In business-to-business, the telemarketer is most often "selling" the prospect on agreeing to receive the business-oriented premium, which starts the marketing conversation.

Here's how the strategy is modified to fit business-to-business.

Step 1. Introduction
Step 2. Get Attention
Step 3. Qualify
Step 4. Present Benefits and State the Offer
Step 5. Ask for the Order
Step 6. Repeat Steps Three to Five

Here's how the marketing conversation might proceed in a cold business-to-business call:

1. Introduction   **Caller:** Hello. My name is _____, and I'm calling on behalf of Consolidated Server Software. Thanks for taking my call. Can you hear me?
Prospect: Yes

2. Get Attention   **Caller:** We've just published a 50-page *Guide to Server Software*, and I'd like to send you a copy. It's an analytical report on server performance metrics, and it features benchmark comparisons of all the major programs.

3. Qualify   **Caller:** Are you involved in specifying server software for your company?
Prospect: Yes. Is this another one of those puff pieces?

4. Benefits & Offer   **Caller:** We are as concerned as you are about wasting your time. That's why this report is completely objective in its analysis and offers very clear comparisons of all the major programs. It was put together for us by an independent software-testing laboratory.

5. Ask for Order Caller: I'd like to send you one right now and follow up in a week or so to get your reaction to it. OK?
Prospect: We're not going to change our server program. My technical people really know how to tweak it.

6. Repeat 2–4   **Caller:** Yes, I understand you wouldn't want to make a change unless you were convinced it would be good for business to do so. I'd like to send you this objective 50-page report for your review. You can mark it up and send it around to your technical people. What server software do you use?

Prospect: We use MegaServer.

Caller: I've talked with a number of organizations that are using MegaServer and they say they are impressed with the way the technical specs are laid out in our 50-page report. I'd like to send you a copy right now and follow up to get your reaction. OK?

In fact, you can see from this sample conversation that business-to-business may not be as conducive to scripting as business-to-consumer conversations. Business-to-business is often a good application for the call guide, because it tends to use a small range of products for which the telemarketer needs to have fairly in-depth knowledge. It is often done in-house as well.

Nonlive Telemarketing

Some businesses have begun to use nonlive telemarketing. It can be difficult to get results with this approach, but the costs are so low that almost any results can justify it, at least financially.

There are two main types of nonlive telemarketing. The first is a recorded pitch that typically asks the listener to respond by calling back to a toll-free number. Some telemarketers using this approach call during the day to target answering machines. They know that most people, on arriving home, press the "Play" button on the machine and wander about doing little errands while they listen to the messages. Since they are often too far away from the machine to hit the "Forward" button, they hear the whole message, even though they might not care to.

Many telemarketers use recorded messages with the aim of connecting directly with people. If the offer is sufficiently compelling and presented early in the pitch, it can be effective, and it's a lot cheaper than using human beings to make the outbound calls. There may be some prospects who like the novelty of one-way communication in a two-way medium.

The other type of nonlive call is based on new technology that has emerged recently: interactive voice messaging. Consumers receive prerecorded messages as described above, much like personally delivered radio spots. However, there's a built-in response mechanism. They can then choose to respond via the touchpad on their phone. The cost-saving benefit to the marketing company is that they can now reach thousands of customers at once.

Like so many of the communications options we mention in this book, interactive voice messaging is most appropriate—and definitely most effective—when you are communicating with your current customers. In fact, utilizing any prerecorded or non-live telemarketing as an acquisition sales tool will probably be ineffective and may very well alienate the prospects you are trying to reach.

Remember, our point in making this warning, and, indeed, our point throughout the book is this: conversations are most effective when both parties want to participate. With that said, you may want to consider interactive voice messaging when you need to leave a "courtesy" message, invitation, service reminder, or any other respectful solicitation.

Depending on the nature of your message, you can time delivery to reach a live customer, enabling them to respond to your offer in "real time." You also can send the message when you are likely to catch voicemail or an answering machine. Business associations, for example, may broadcast a reminder to seminar participants after hours. The professional receives the voicemail the next day, appreciates the reminder, and also appreciates that he or she did not have to interrupt their day to speak to a live representative.

If executed well, these messages can contain a sense of the same personal touch and warmth of a real person. It's a good idea, for example, to select the appropriate voiceover talent for your message just as you would for a television or radio spot. Meanwhile, the technology's interactivity allows your customer to respond. They can accept or decline an offer or be connected to a live representative.

One company that has pioneered this new technology is Burlington, Massachusetts-based SoundBite Communications. SoundBite's clients represent many Global 2000 companies who have taken advantage of the medium for applications such as boosting response to a direct mailing, allowing "one-touch" subscription renewals, sending customer alerts and reminders, conducting automated polling, and more.

Industries for which this technology is most appropriate include:

- Political parties, non-profits and member-based organizations
- Subscription publishing companies
- Event planners
- Financial services
- Telecommunications, ISPs, cable and broadband services
- Utilities
- Travel and hospitality

Again, this medium has proven most valuable when targeting current customers, current members, or people who have opted-in, and when used in concert with other communications. In fact, SoundBite claims to have lifted response rates of other media by thirty to five hundred percent simply by adding one of their voice messages to the mix.

Is Telemarketing for You?

Despite current opinions and regulations, telemarketing, if conducted professionally and respectfully, can be an effective marketing tool. There are instances in which marketers have abused the medium and violated the privacy, preferences, and trust of potential customers.

There are also, however, great success stories in both business-to-consumer and business-to-business applications.

Careful selection of your list and technology, along with the appropriate training of your telemarketing staff can help you implement a successful campaign and create or enhance a positive experience for your customers.

Notes

1. Robert Doscher and Richard Simms, *The DialAmerica Teleservices Handbook*, (Lincolnwood, IL: NTC Business Books, 2001, 41).

Radio

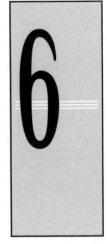

It's Halloween, 1938, and at precisely eight p.m., Orson Welles and his Mercury Theater air their legendary *War of the Worlds* broadcast.

Six million Americans have gathered around their radios as the CBS announcer introduces the play. Some of them aren't listening too closely, and some tune in late. They hear not a play, but the dance music of Ramon Raquello and his orchestra, live from the Park Plaza Hotel in New York City. Suddenly, a reporter interrupts with a news bulletin of an explosion on Mars. A few minutes later, there's another bulletin, and then another. A spaceship loaded with tentacled creatures has landed in Grovers Mill, New Jersey. Martians are blasting the populace with deadly heat rays and releasing a toxic black gas over the countryside.

At this point, listeners begin to panic. Police switchboards are swamped with calls. People load their cars with food and blankets, hoping to outrun the poison gas or hide in their cellars waiting for it to blow over.

Forty minutes into the program, there is another announcement that the broadcast is only a play. This announcement is repeated twice more during the show, but somehow it doesn't sink in with the listeners. Hundreds of thousands of them remain convinced their country is under attack.

"Interesting story," you might say. "But what does something that happened more than sixty years ago have to do with today's marketing?" "Plenty," according to copywriter and script writer Jean Hall of Norwood, Massachusetts. This anecdote vividly illustrates both the strengths and weaknesses of radio as an advertising medium.

As Dorothy Thompson, a *New York Tribune* columnist, noted at the time, "Mr. Orson Welles and the Mercury Theater . . . have proved that a few effective voices, accompanied by sound effects, can convince masses of people of a totally unreasonable, completely fantastic proposition."

Of course, what you're trying to get across to your audience isn't unreasonable or fantastic at all. What you're trying to convey are the virtues of the product or service your company or your client is pinning their hopes on. But, Jean Hall reminds us, you can still use *War of the Worlds* tactics in the battle for your target audience's hearts and pocketbooks and give yourself and your clients a huge competitive advantage by doing so.

Radio as an Advertising Medium

Suppose the folks in R&D have just come up with a terrific Tahitian tanning formula and you want sun worshipers to call in for a free sample. You could just tell your listeners about its advantages—and get nothing more than a giant yawn for your troubles. Instead, Hall suggests, why not take them to Tahiti and let them bask on the sunny white beaches and dip their toes in the azure waters while you convince them that your tanning formula is superior to others?

If you were running a television commercial or print ad, you could do that with the proverbial picture that's worth a thousand words. Unfortunately, the location shoot to get that picture is going to cost you plenty.

With radio, however, you can accomplish the same thing for a fraction of the budget. All you need is the sound of ocean waves lapping on the shore and the rhythm of tropical drums beating in the background while a suitably sultry voice extols your tanning breakthrough.

And the best part is, with the proper encouragement, listeners will fill in a setting that's more lush and more appealing than anything a location scout could find because if you've hooked your listeners with your sounds and your story, they're working with something more powerful than the best camera lens. Jean Hall is one of the best marketing copywriters in the business but she also knows that in addition to her writing, her radio listeners are *participating in the process with their imaginations.*

Even the most talented special-effects whiz can't create aliens or monsters as scary as those in our heads. The scene your listeners envision for themselves can be more engaging and more effective than any pre-packaged visual you can create. What's more, radio not only lets you take your audience anywhere in the world, it allows you to transport them to other worlds, go time traveling, and paint landscapes that couldn't possibly exist.

You can conjure up a forest of lollipops to sell a children's magazine, or introduce Albert Einstein to Attila the Hun and let them compare notes on your accounting software. You can even use sound bites from a music collection or video series to take listeners back to their high school days or to the front lines of the D-Day Invasion.

What radio can't do—and this was what caused problems with the *War of the Worlds* broadcast—is keep an important point constantly before the audience. During the *War of the Worlds* broadcast, people became so engrossed in the drama that they simply didn't hear or else forgot the fact that it was only a play.

Hall emphasizes that on the radio, you have to keep repeating your company name, even if it seems a little awkward at first. Recap your offer and drum that important web site or phone number into their ears, especially near the end of the spot, because there are no on-screen "supers" to remind them.

With a few exceptions, such as a music collection, another thing radio can't do is demonstrate your product. Radio can't provide close-up shots to show why your product costs more than that of your competitors. This is why many savvy marketers use radio for lead generation, rather than for closing the sale.

Now that we've covered a little about what radio can and cannot do, let's take a look at how some of today's top marketers are using radio to maximum advantage, and examine some new trends that could make your own efforts even more effective.

Announcer-Read Radio

Perhaps you're wondering if radio will work for you, but you don't want to spend a fortune to find out. Maybe you've tried traditionally produced radio, but found the price tag hard to swallow. If so, announcer-read commercials may be a solution because of the economy, flexibility, and other advantages they offer.

To find out more about this type of direct response radio, we spoke to Gary Kretchmer, Vice President of Target + Response Marketing, Inc. in Chicago, who cited some of the pros and cons of announcer-read radio.

On the positive side, production costs are zero. Since you're using personnel and facilities that the station provides free to get your business, there are no bills for studio time or union talent. You pay only copywriting charges and other agency fees.

Additionally, with announcer-read radio, the delivery of your spots matches the sound of the stations they're running on. For example, you've chosen to air on a rock station and on a classical station or on a station in Boston and a station in Dallas. There's no need to produce a generic commercial that tries to be all things to all people or to create different versions so your message is appropriate for each audience. The announcer's accent and tone of voice, as well as any music that's laid in behind the voice will always be appropriate to the station's audience. What's more, your copy can be customized easily to refer to specific locations, address listeners as New Englanders or Texans, and cover the special concerns of listeners in each area.

Finally, announcer-read radio lets you respond immediately to important events or changing market conditions. Suppose you're in the roof replacement business, and there's a torrential rainstorm in one of your markets. You can send new copy to the stations in that area via fax, and have a new spot on air as fast as one of their announcers can get to the microphone.

What kind of creative approach works best with announcer-read radio? Most of the rules we'll be discussing later with regard to produced radio also apply here: a strong opening, repetition of the phone number and product name, and so on. But, there are also a few additional things that can make your announcer-read spots more effective.

To start, you need to remember what kind of spot you're writing. Since your commercial will be delivered by a station announcer, it's wise to keep the tone of the copy conversational, so it sounds as though it's being said, not read.

Using humor with announcer-read spots can be a tricky proposition, so use it selectively. Some announcers may find it hard to find the right tone and you won't be there to direct them. As a spot for FreeCreditReport.com illustrates later in this chapter, humor can be used effectively as long as it reinforces, rather than distracts from, your message.

Finally, to prevent errors, it's a good idea to phonetically spell unfamiliar or difficult to pronounce words in your copy.

Per Inquiry Radio

Despite all the savings announcer-read radio offers, you may still be a little nervous about committing to a full-blown campaign or a test because of the media costs. If so, there's another option you can use with both announcer-read spots and produced spots, (discussed later in this chapter). That option is per inquiry (PI) radio.

With this method, you minimize your financial risk because you know in advance exactly how much each inquiry or order is going to cost you. Here's how it works.

You set your maximum allowable cost per inquiry and/or your maximum allowable cost per order. You give these figures to the stations you're interested in running on, and they let you know whether or not they'll air your spots. Then, when the switchboard starts lighting up, you pay the agreed-upon amount.

Obviously, stations are interested in making as much money as possible, and they can do that in one of two ways. One, by generating thousands of orders for a relatively inexpensive item like a $19.95 compact disk, or two, by generating a smaller number of orders for a high-ticket item like a three thousand dollar cabinet refinishing job, which has substantially higher "allowables."

Not surprisingly, consumers may be a bit leery of paying three thousand dollars for something they can't see on the non-visual medium of radio, especially since they're hearing only a thirty or sixty second description of it. That's why with high-ticket items, radio usually works better for lead generation than for direct sales. In this kind of two-step process, you might offer a free estimate for home-improvement projects such as vinyl siding or replacement windows, a free thirty-day trial of your computer software, or a newsletter for people with a specific medical condition.

Per inquiry radio has a strong track record of success for financial and investment services, where an initial phone call can turn into a highly profitable long-term relationship. And, because you can amortize your allowables over more than one purchase or gift, it can be an excellent choice for continuity products like a series of books on the Civil War or monthly gifts to sponsor a needy child in a foreign country. Gary Kretchmer, whose firm specializes in per inquiry radio, offers a couple of excellent tips for making any of these offers successful.

What works best, Kretchmer has found, is to "pick an enemy." By this, he doesn't mean a person you dislike or even your most aggressive competitor. Your enemy should be a problem your listeners have that can be solved by your product or service. Don't select any problem, select the most dramatic one you can.

For instance, take the case of E-Trade Bank, a financial institution that is able to offer higher rates on CDs and money market funds because it does not have the overhead of brick-and-mortar locations. For this client, Kretchmer picked the recent volatility of the stock market as the enemy. "The Dow is up. The Dow is down," his script began, and then it went on to show listeners how they could get a better return on their money than they could at their local bank without exposing themselves to the risks they might encounter on Wall Street.

Kretchmer also stresses that a unique selling proposition is essential to set you apart from the also-rans. "Personalized service" isn't going to do it. Everybody says that, whether they've got it or not. What you need is a feature or benefit that is yours and yours alone. Lacking this, select an attribute one or two other companies may share but have not claimed by making it a cornerstone of their advertising.

Find that advantage and keep driving it home. If you're the biggest, oldest, or fastest-growing in your industry, enhance your credibility by saying so. In today's competitive environment, "me too" products just won't generate the calls you're looking for.

Produced Radio

Earlier in this chapter, we discussed announcer-read radio advertising and the advantages it can offer. Another option is to produce and distribute pre-recorded radio spots. While this approach requires a bigger budget than that for announcer-read spots, it has many unique advantages and, when executed properly, can often be even more effective.

What are the additional costs involved? This depends on the types of concepts you've decided on and how complicated they are to execute.

First, you'll need to budget for talent, the voices that will be heard in your spot. Many pre-recorded radio spots feature just one voice and involve a very straightforward, "announcer" type of read.

Other radio concepts require two or more distinct voices, sometimes to add variety to a straight-announcer spot, sometimes to create a "slice-of-life" conversation, or sometimes to play characters in a thirty- or sixty-second mini-drama.

Regardless of why you're using them, multi-voice commercials are going to be more expensive to produce than single-voice spots because of the additional talent you'll have to pay. To get the right voices, you'll need to allow sufficient time for casting.

Casting can be done in person if you have a budget big enough to hire a casting firm or if you're going to use the same talent for radio as you will for a television spot or campaign. A more economical option is to request and listen to casting tapes from major talent agencies. These tapes usually include several different types of spots by each announcer the agency represents and can be a big help in making your decision. If you'd like to get an even better idea of how your finished spot will sound, you can look into the possibility of getting an audition tape where one or more announcers read scripts you've faxed the talent agency.

Other costs associated with produced radio spots include the cost of the sound engineer and the facility you're going to use to record and mix the spots, as well as fees for any music and sound effects you wish to include. The studio may be able to supply these, or you may want to use a specialist to search for them. In any event, listen to them beforehand, so you're sure you've got what you want and don't have to spend expensive studio time searching for something else.

You'll also need to budget for a qualified professional to direct the session and bring out the best performances from the talent you've hired. Additionally, you will need to budget for the cost of producing and shipping the "dubs" (copies of the spot that you'll be sending to the client and the stations, as well as keeping on file yourself).

While these costs add up to a radio spot that is more expensive than an announcer-read script, production costs are still considerably less than those for a similar concept executed for television. When well done, produced radio spots can have powerful advantages over announcer-read spots.

For one thing, radio is a great story-telling medium, and produced radio spots can break through the clutter with compelling stories and characters. While straightforward announcer-read spots are great at presenting rational sales arguments, produced spots can tap into the imagination of the listening audience and create dramatic situations with which the listener can identify and relate. As a result, produced radio spots have more power to move the listener emotionally.

Produced radio spots also give you a level of control that announcer-read spots can't because they're distributed to radio stations only after they've been approved by the agency and client.

To make sure everybody agrees, and that you don't have to go back and re-record the spot, it's essential to have an agency writer, producer, or creative director on hand to direct the spot or assist the independent producer/director you've hired. In many instances, you'll also want a client representative at the session to provide additional input and who has the power to give final approval. Everyone should be made aware that all comments should be funneled through the director to avoid wasting time and confusing the talent.

Having the right people at the session allows you not only to coax the best acting performances from your talent, but to ensure that the finished spot delivers the best performance from an advertising perspective, too. For example, you'll be able to control what words to emphasize in each sentence and, perhaps more important, the kind of tone you'll use to best support your sales argument.

Should the voice that listeners hear be authoritative or friendly, sarcastic or inquisitive? The answer can be important to the success of your spots, and produced radio gives you the power to make sure you're satisfied before the spots air.

Last but not least, produced radio spots allow you to take a successful television concept and integrate it into your radio advertising.

Consider the example of FreeCreditReport.com, which recently ran a direct response television spot featuring a lovable, animated "stick figure" character. The television spot was a hit and went into a major national roll-out. You'll see an example of this in Chapter Seven.

When the animated television spot first aired, FreeCreditReport.com was running a series of radio spots that were totally unrelated to the television spot. They decided to quickly test a similar concept on radio, and used the same company that produced the television spot, Auster Productions, of Los Angeles, California, to handle radio production, as well. Jean Hall wrote the script.

Figure 6.1: Sample Radio Script

CLIENT: FreeCreditReport.com
AGENCY: The Response Shop, Inc.

FreeCreditReport.com
:60 radio
"When?"

TICK-TOCK MUSIC, FADING UNDER
ANNCR: When was the last time you checked your credit report? Were Beanie Babies the hot new trend? Were people dancing the Macarena? Was George Bush president? The *other* George Bush? You say you've *never* checked your credit report? You know, experts say you should do it regularly. And now's the perfect time to start. Because it's never been easier, thanks to FreeCreditReport.com. Just log onto FreeCreditReport.com, and we'll show you how to get a free credit report right online. See the information lenders and credit card companies use to help them make their decisions. Check for negative entries and possible inaccuracies. And get 30 days of our CreditCheck® Monitoring Service at no obligation. Don't put it off any longer.

Log onto FreeCreditReport.com today. FreeCreditReport.com. Because if you haven't checked your credit report since Dallas won the Super Bowl—it's been *way* too long.

Here's what Sam Auster, director, had to say about the campaign: "By leveraging a creative concept that was proven in TV, we ended up with a big win in radio, too. We used the same basic script structure and characters in the radio spots, and the same voice talents. By integrating voice, music, and sound effects that evoked the TV spots, we were able to build on what we had already achieved, and make both media even more effective."

What are some of the keys to developing successful produced radio spots?

Get Personal Great radio advertising leverages the intimate nature of radio to engage the audience in a one-on-one dialogue. The FreeCreditReport.com radio spot discussed in Figure 6.1 is a good example of this. The spot opens with "When was the last time you checked your credit report?" The spot goes on to inform listeners that there's one way to find out, by logging on to FreeCreditReport.com.

Not only does this spot grab the listener's attention immediately by speaking directly to them, but it also utilizes the tried-and-true problem/solution approach.

Be Specific Avoid empty claims like "we're the best." Generic claims aren't believed, and they won't differentiate you from the competition. Instead, focus on what makes you unique. Include support points in your copy that reinforce the main benefit.

Keep It Simple Producing a radio spot that is nothing but wall-to-wall copy is one of the most common mistakes that advertisers new to radio make. The fast-talking pace turns listeners off, and even if they do listen they won't remember anything after the spot ends. Radio is not a visual medium; less is more. Don't try to do too much and try to repeat key information as often as possible. If you're worried that you won't be able to include all the information a prospect needs to make a purchase decision, consider structuring your offer as a two-step lead-generation effort.

Urgency Works You've got your listeners interested in your product, maybe even excited about it. They may think there's plenty of time to respond. So, how do you keep them from putting off ordering or forgetting all about it? Give them a deadline. Make that special discount available to the next X-number of callers only. Or tell your audience this is a limited-time offer and give them an expiration date, one that gives them time to act but lets them know if they wait too long they'll miss out. You can even extend your deadline once, citing the "terrific demand," but don't overdo it. If there's never a week or two when your "limited-time offer" isn't available, people will notice and will know you aren't serious.

Make a Tempting Offer Even without a specific deadline, the use of a compelling offer imparts a sense of urgency. Despite what you might hear in focus groups, "free" is still the most powerful word in the English language. To give your radio campaign its best chance of success, make sure you make your audience "an offer they can't refuse."

Endorsement Radio

It's Monday morning, and you're stuck in traffic on the way to your office. You have other things on your mind besides Chicago gridlock, because, like millions of others, you're listening to "The Don & Roma Show." As they have on many other Monday mornings, they're talking about the leisurely weekend they spent on their boat on Lake Michigan.

You've listened to their show for years, and you feel like you know them. Roma is always saying how she likes to keep things clean, so you're not surprised when she starts talking about how hard it is to get the mildew and stains out of the boat's carpet and upholstery. It's a *problem she's been battling for years. But this time, she's got good news.* She's discovered the Sharper Image Steam Wizard. And she goes on to explain more about it and tell listeners how they can try it for themselves.

Was that a commercial or advice from a trusted source, based on actual use of the product? When you're listening to "endorsement radio," you're listening to both paid commercial advertising and advice from a real user of the product.

Just what is endorsement radio, and how does it work? To find the answers, we talked to the foremost experts on the subject, Dave and Patty Newmark. Their firm, Newmark Advertising of Encino, California, places more of this kind of advertising than any other agency.

According to Dave, endorsement commercials by radio hosts have enormous potential to influence the purchasing behavior of radio personalities' loyal audiences. "By borrowing on the hosts' credibility with their listeners," he says, "endorsement commercials seem more like word-of mouth recommendations than actual commercials."

"In fact, research tells us that almost half of the listeners don't realize it's a commercial," adds Patty, "and that's one of the reasons this kind of advertising is so effective."

Sounds simple. In fact, these programs are anything but simple to execute properly. There's a lot of research behind successful implementation because radio is a local medium, and there are hundreds of radio shows and personalities in major markets across the country.

"Success in this area goes way beyond audience demographics—or ratings," Dave explains. "The radio host has to be a good fit for the products and its audience. Having in-depth, accurate biographical information on the various hosts is an absolute necessity. To that end, we maintain a database of biographical data on the hosts. We include as much lifestyle information as we can get. Is the host a smoker? Has he ever struggled with a weight problem? Is he married?"

All this information is important, because one of the keys of successful endorsement radio is having a host who is willing to try the product at least once and then to talk about it sincerely.

"One of the first things we do is ask the host to try the product and talk to us about their experience. We do this before we commit to a deal," says Dave. "And you have to be willing to walk away if you don't like what you hear."

Once a host is identified and a deal negotiated, there's still plenty to do, for example, educating the host on the product and providing guidance on key messages. It's important that the hosts sound natural and not scripted. The spots need to sound spontaneous, specific, and genuine.

Quality control is another part of the process. As part of the agreement, each station must tape all the airings and post them to a web site. Someone at Newmark then listens to every single spot, every day, to check the quality.

"Because execution is so critical to the success of these programs, they need to be carefully monitored and continually adjusted. These programs are 'high-touch' in every sense of the word," says Dave. "We provide feedback and coaching to the hosts whenever necessary."

For a number of high-profile clients like Proflowers.com and Intuit, makers of TurboTax software, endorsement radio has paid off handsomely. This choice, however, is not for everyone. While this approach does not have the production expenses associated with pre-recorded radio spots, it does require you to pay ongoing talent fees to the radio personalities based on how many times the spot airs. Over time, this can become expensive. You may find that other types of radio are more cost-effective for your particular business.

Finding the Right Solution

What type of radio will work best for you? The economy and flexibility of announcer-read radio? The limitless creative possibilities and enhanced control of produced radio? The intimate persuasion of endorsement radio?

There's no hard-and-fast rule. The only way to find out is through testing. By carefully evaluating the merits of each creative approach and the cost-effectiveness of each campaign, you'll learn more and more about what works for your particular product or service, and how to make the *War of the Worlds* medium of radio a powerful weapon in your marketing arsenal.

Television

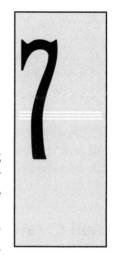

A gerbil being shot out of a cannon. A man being rushed into the emergency room with money "out the wazoo." A naked man answering the door for a pizza delivery.

Remember all those dot-coms spots from a few years ago? More importantly, do you remember *responding* to any of those television spots? If your answer is no, Marla Hoskins, President of The Response Shop *(www.response-lab.com)*, a La Jolla, California agency that specializes in direct response television, isn't surprised. Many of those companies are now out of business. And one reason is that they spent millions of dollars on television advertising that didn't work. While viewers may have noticed their spots, they didn't feel compelled to *act* on them.

That's a real shame because direct response television with a response vehicle can work well, extraordinarily well, according to Hoskins. But only if it's the *right kind* of television: television that's based on a solid strategic foundation and uses proven direct response techniques.

So what can you do to give *your* spot a chance of succeeding? Let's start with understanding what television is, and how it differs from other media.

Television as an Advertising Medium

Television can be used to build awareness of your product or service, and get people to remember your name. It can create brand preference. But television can do more than get people to just remember your name or prefer your brand. Television can utilize a direct response mechanism with the *primary goal* of driving traffic to your web site, call center, or mailing address, and convincing potential customers to *immediately* buy or request more information.

If you've ever purchased a music collection from Time-Life Music, called for a free quote on auto insurance from Unitrin Direct, or typed LendingTree.com into your web browser as a result of watching a television spot, then you can count yourself among the millions of consumers who've responded to the temptations of a television marketing conversation

Key Creative Strategy Strengths

Many of the techniques that are employed in television are similar to those used in the print media. Television, however, offers some tools to the direct marketer that print media do not. In order to maximize your success on television, you'll need to master all of the key creative strengths that make television different from print media.

Rule #1: Use Sight *and Sound* to Maximum Advantage

Although some networks will run two-minute spots, most direct response commercials are sixty-seconds in length. That's not a lot of time to get a message across, so it's important to leverage not only sight, but *sound* to maximum advantage.

Don't forget that many in the audience are passive viewers; the television is *on*, but it may not have anyone's full *attention*. In order to get your message across, you have to do something in the first few seconds of the spot that will get them to stop everything else they're doing and go into "active viewing" mode. And you don't have to rely merely on words and images to do this. The right voice, music, and sound effects can also help grab the audience's attention and drive your point home.

Ditech.com is one advertiser that uses sound effects to its advantage: One of its spots opens with a flashing, on-screen graphic that says "Mortgage Alert," accompanied by a loud siren (sound effect). Words alone would not grab your attention nearly as well.

A recent Matrix Direct spot opens with a newspaper landing on a stoop with a loud "thud." The headline on the newspaper reads "Great Rates on Quality Term Life Insurance." An authoritative-sounding announcer opens the spot with this line: "Here's *big news* on term life insurance!" As if this wasn't already enough to grab the viewer's attention, the message was further enhanced by a terrific choice of music, a track called "Headline News" from stock music house Mega-Trax. The total effect was a very newsy, important-sounding opening.

Rule #2: If It's Important, *Super It!* Studies have shown that the average person comprehends better and retains more when they *read* something, than when they *hear* it. It's not enough to *say* "Special Introductory Offer" or "Save 50%," you need to reinforce that message with *on-screen graphics*. With direct mail, a prospect can always double back and re-read a section if they find that they are confused. Television viewers can't do this. In order to ensure that your message is understood, you need on-screen graphics to reinforce key selling points. Don't be afraid to use large graphics, with bold, intrusive colors. Repeat key messages at least once.

Rule #3: If It's *Really* Important: Animate It! Thanks to recent innovations in technology, it's easier than ever to create motion graphics. Use them to your advantage. Don't just super your special offer, *animate it!* Have the words fly in from left to right. Have one image explode to reveal another. Have some fun with motion graphics by using a combination of message, motion and sound effects as "punctuators."

Marla Hoskins, of The Response Shop, has this to say: "We rarely go into an edit bay anymore without our motion graphics artist. For example, we recently did a spot for AOL to promote Version 9.0 with TopSpeed™ Technology. The spot ends with the traditional direct response call-to-action and end tag. But right in the middle of the end tag, we had AOL's "running man" tear into the scene on a motorcycle and pop a wheelie, complete with Harley Davidson sound effects. It really tied together the main message of the spot (speed)—and the brand identity in a memorable way." (To see the spot in its entirety, go to www.response-lab.com).

Rule #4: Seeing Is Believing! One of the truly great things about television is its ability to *demonstrate* a product. Television allows you to *prove* that your product is easy-to-use, not just to *claim* it. Television's power to demonstrate has always been put to good use by savvy direct marketers—just think of all of the infomercials for exercise programs and kitchen gadgets. But in the past 10 years, the power of using direct response and television has been discovered by a new generation of marketers to promote high tech products. For example, Intuit, maker of TurboTax software, provides a demonstration of its award-winning "EasyStep™ Interview" process in its television spots. The on-screen demonstration does more to convince prospects of the product's ease-of-use than any words in a direct mail package or on a retail box ever could!

For some products, the *audio track* is the product demonstration. Just consider what Mitch Peyser, Vice President of Marketing at Time-Life Music, has to say: "Our audio track serves several purposes in our spots. So, it's important that we play as many songs as possible. Naturally, the audio track gets people excited about the music. But the audio track is also our proof to viewers that the collection really *does* have all the great songs they remember. The more songs we can play in the spot's audio track, the better. It's also our way of establishing that what we're selling includes only *original hits* by the *original artists,* not re-records. All of these points are very important to our audience. As a result, in our spots you'll actually hear very little announcer 'sell copy' and lots of music in the clear."

Rule #5: Happy Customers Attract New Customers

Testimonials are a powerful tool in any medium in which they are used. But testimonials in television are doubly effective, because television captures not just the *message* content, but the *emotional* content, as well. Says award-winning infomercial writer Paul Allen: "Testimonials allow viewers to experience surrogate benefits. Keep in mind that as a television marketer you're trying to convince someone to buy a product that they can't actually try or touch before they order it. Testimonials allow prospects to see real people, people *just like them,* experiencing your product."

There is no better way to connect with an audience than to use *real people*, expressing *real feelings and experiences,* about your product!

Now that we've covered what makes television so powerful, let's move on to talk about other ways to cut through the clutter, and get your message heard.

Television Tactics: Opening Hooks

Many of the same tactics that are employed in print media apply to television. In direct mail, your first task is to get the envelope opened. You simply have no chance of selling anything to anyone unless you do that.

The primary goal of the first five to ten seconds of a television spot is to get someone to watch the rest of your spot. No one watches television just for the commercials; in fact, in many homes where the television is on, no one is watching television, it's merely playing as a background element to other activities, like housework or homework. So, you have to have a strategy to get someone to stop what they are doing and actually *listen* to your message. Here are a few techniques you can use to do just that.

Tactic #1: Make a Dramatic Statement One way to immediately engage an audience is to open your spot with a dramatic statement. The statement can be about almost anything, including your product, your audience, or even your offer.

Check out this spot opener, from Fairfield Resorts: "Here's the deal-of-a-lifetime on a dream getaway for you and your family to magical Orlando! Now you can treat your family to four fun-filled days and three magnificent nights in Orlando, for just $198 per package!"

Earlier in this chapter, we talked about a Matrix Direct spot that opens with an authoritative-sounding announcer making this statement: "Here's *big news* on term life insurance!" Why does this opening get your attention? Because when someone announces that they have big news, it's human nature to keep listening, at least until the listener decides for himself or herself if the message lives up to its hype!

PrivacyGuard™, a service that helps protect consumers against identity theft, opens its spot with film noir style footage of a mysterious figure typing at a desk. The camera then moves into an extreme close-up of the words he has typed, "Identity Theft," as the following announcer voice over (v/o) lines are delivered:

Anncr:	Identity theft is the fastest-growing crime in America. Somebody uses *your* social security number, and the IRS could bill *you* for the taxes. Somebody gets a credit card in *your* name, and huge charges start showing up . . . "

It's not easy to ignore an opening hook like that.

Tactic #2: Ask a Question Why do questions work as opening hooks? For one thing, the subject of a question is *you!* And, an opening question gets the viewer to start thinking about the subject matter being discussed and the personal experience with it. Think of opening a spot with a question as television's equivalent to an involvement device in direct mail.

An animated FreeCreditReport.com spot opens with a couple of stick figure characters power-walking. The announcer v/o asks: "Got big plans for the future? A new car? College for the kids? Maybe a dream vacation?" The spot immediately gets consumers to identify with the characters. After all, who doesn't have big plans for the future? The announcer then goes on to link having big plans for the future with being credit-ready, and with knowing what's in your credit report.

A Christian Children's Fund television spot opens with this copy:

Man, Speaking to Camera:	How many people have made a difference in *your* life? A teacher? A friend? A boss you once had? Maybe someone you didn't even know made a *huge* difference in your life by *believing in you*. Giving you a break when you never expected it . . .

A recent life insurance spot opens with this question: "Are you paying too much for life insurance?" The video shows a close-up of a pair of hands counting out twenty dollar bills. The spot goes on to urge viewers to call and get a free quote, and possibly save hundreds of dollars a year. Why does this opening work? Let's face it, nobody likes to think that somebody else is getting a better deal! Fear of paying too much is a great consumer motivator, and a perennial favorite in television spots.

Tactic #3: Pique Their Curiosity Another tried-and-true way to open a television spot is by piquing the viewers' curiosity.

Consider this example: A beautiful, animated television spot for Gevalia Kaffe opens with a female announcer with a very sensual voice making this statement: "You sense it when it arrives . . . ."

Why does this opening hook work? Answer: Because it leverages consumer psychology. After all, when you hear someone talking about "it," you want to keep listening long enough to find out what "it" is!

A Unitrin Direct auto insurance spot opens with this hook "You'll find them in every town, city, and suburb across all of Florida. Different people of different ages, from different walks of life, that all share the same belief . . . "

Tactic #4: Give 'Em the Silent Treatment If you really want to grab someone's attention on television, try a whisper, or even silence! A very compelling spot by IDT Long Distance opens up with a male announcer v/o whispering: "Shhhh! Want to know a secret?" What follows is the sound of typing. On the screen, a type-written message appears one letter at a time, beginning with this sentence, "All long distance is pretty much the same, except the price!" Except for the one opening announcer v/o line, one closing announcer v/o line, and the typewriter sound effects, *the spot is completely silent.*

A spot for Unitrin Direct, a car insurance business opens this way:

Anncr:	If you have one of *these*
	SHOT OF AUTOMOBILE LICENSE PLATE
Anncr:	You could save lots of *this*
	SHOT OF HAND HOLDING $20 BILLS

Anncr:	By using one of *these* . . .
	SHOT OF TELEPHONE
Anncr:	. . . to call Unitrin Direct!
	CUT TO UNITRIN LOGO

The key words "car," "money," and "telephone" are not voiced. The announcer's inflection indicates to the listener that he has something he wants you to *look at*.

The technique works precisely as it was intended to work: We look at the screen to find out what's going on.

Tactic #5: Use a Screening Statement or Question

Television is most effective when reaching a mass audience. However, it can sometimes be used very effectively to reach a smaller, more defined audience. Consider the case of eHealthInsurance, Inc., an online broker of health insurance. Who do they want their television spot to address? You only have to listen to the spot for a few seconds to find out:

Anncr:	"If you're paying too much for health insurance without getting the benefits you need, or you haven't got health insurance at all—Listen! You could be getting better benefits, for less, through eHealth.com! eHealth.com is the fastest, easiest way for individuals, families and small businesses to shop, compare and *save* on quality health insurance."

Another great example of using a screening statement as an opener is provided by Advanta Mortgage:

Anncr:	Do you need cash but are worried about getting *the right deal?*
	If you need cash—to pay off bills, for home improvements or just to spend as you like—and you want the loan set up on *your* terms—call this toll free number *now* . . . .

Tactic #6: Make an Analogy Another great way to open a spot and get a point across is by making an analogy. This can be particularly effective when promoting a product or category that is relatively new and unfamiliar.

Eva Boker, Senior Vice President of Marketing at LowerMyBills, offered this comment about the unique marketing challenges they faced: "We're not selling a product; we're selling a service. So, there are no 'beauty shots' to build a spot around. Furthermore, the service we sell can be hard to describe. So, we chose to set up a classic problem/solution situation, using a lovable animated character. We used the character to create an analogy between the ease and convenience of shopping in a grocery store, and the ease and convenience of shopping for home loans, car insurance, and other consumer services at

Figure 7.1: Comparison Shopping, LowerMyBills.com, The Response Shop.

Reprinted with permission of The Response Shop and LowerMyBills.com.

Check out the "Comparison Shopping" animated spot created by The Response Shop for LowerMyBills.com.

LowerMyBills.com. We felt that the analogy was key to getting across the benefits of shopping at LowerMyBills.com, and animation was key to getting the idea across in an engaging way."

Tactic #7: Dispel a Myth Citibank is one of a number of television advertisers who use the "dispel a myth" opening. One of their spots promoting the Citibank AAdvantage World MasterCard opens with a couple in a department store shopping for luggage. An off-camera announcer begins the dialogue:

Anncr:	Hi. Interested in earning free airline miles?
Woman:	Sure!
Anncr:	Think you don't fly enough to earn them?
Man & Woman:	Yes.
Anncr:	Think miles are good only on one airline?
Man & Woman::	Mh-hm
Anncr:	Think again! Every day, more people are flying to more places, *free . . .*

The announcer goes on to explain that you can earn miles on *everyday purchases* with the Citibank AAdvantage World MasterCard.

Dell uses a similar type of opening in a spot that opens with "Think you can't afford Dell quality on a smaller budget? Think again!"

These spots work because they immediately overcome consumer perceptions that have proven to be barriers to response. They also work because they are terrific examples of immediately engaging the audience by opening with a question.

Tactic #8: Tap into Customer Testimonials Some of the best copy you'll ever put in your television spot will not be written by a copywriter. It will be un-rehearsed, straight from the mouths of your fan club members: your customers.

Trendwest Resorts, a timeshare developer, feels that their best sales people are their customers. So they featured them in an infomercial. Here are some of the delightful owner testimonials that open their thirty-minute show:

| Woman: | I always feel when we're on a vacation with WorldMark that every day is an adventure. There's always something great to do. |
| Man: | We'll go up in the mountains and go sledding. We'll go over the coast and go beachcombing. We take our bikes and go bicycling as a family. We can do everything as a family and everything is right there. |

Sound like the kind of vacations you want to take? It does to us. And there's nothing more engaging than listening to real people share some of their tips for getting more out of life. Next time you're at the water cooler, start talking about your favorite product or service, and see what kind of circle gathers around you.

One other point about infomercials: Because they are thirty minutes in length, their opening hooks are longer than the ten to fifteen second hooks used in short-form television. Count on using the first two to three *minutes* of an infomercial to hook in your audience.

Example: Following the testimonials quoted above, the World-Mark infomercial cuts to sizzling vacation footage, accompanied by this announcer v/o copy:

| Anncr: | Why is it that some people always seem to be able to take better vacations than the rest of us? They get away more often, to better places, with nicer accommodations. You *know* they don't make any more money than you . . . so *how do they do it?* Well, stay tuned, because you're about to find out! |
| Anncr: | In the next half hour, you'll discover the *insider's secret* that has allowed nearly 200,000 smart families to take *more* vacations, *better* vacations . . . AND *for a lot less money!* You'll learn how to stop |

asking, "Can we *afford* a vacation this year?" And instead ask, "Where do we *want* to go?"

Wow. Who doesn't want *that?*

Tactic #9: Give the Viewer a Chance to Eavesdrop

One of FreeCreditReport.com's most successful spots opens with "Psst!" followed by a pause. Why does it grab our attention? Answer: Who doesn't want to eavesdrop? After the pause, the announcer asks "Do you have good credit? Or do you only *think* you have?" The spot then goes on to tell viewers how to check their credit report, for free.

Sports Illustrated opens one of their spots with footage of a Dad knocking on his son's bedroom door. We then see the son scrambling to hide something under his mattress. Here's the dialogue that follows:

Dad:	It's about time you and I had a little talk.
Son:	What's up, Dad?
Dad:	It's about these magazines you've been hiding. Now tell me the truth: Where did they come from?"

With an opening like this, would you continue to watch? We know we would.

Tactic #10: Promise a Major Benefit

Proflowers.com runs television spots primarily around major holidays, like Mother's Day and Easter. When they asked The Response Shop to create a spot for Valentine's Day targeting men, they got a real winner with a spot featuring a large, lovable coach character who opens the spot by promising a major benefit: "Guys, here's the *really big play* that'll make *you* a winner this Valentine's Day . . . . "

Whether you choose to open your spot with an enticing benefit, a thought-provoking analogy, or a dramatic statement, you'll find that spending the time to craft an irresistible opening hook is time well spent.

The next time you watch television, pay particular attention to how the spots open. The more you watch, the more you'll notice the incredible similarities between the techniques used to get outer envelopes opened and the techniques used to pull viewers into television spots.

Television Strategy: Needs Assessment

Before we talk about the various methods television advertisers use to communicate benefits, let's talk a little about different types of *message strategies* used, as they dramatically affect the content and structure of your spot. So, how do you determine what kind of *message strategy* you need?

The best place to start, when thinking about a television spot, is with the mindset of your prospect. What information do they need before deciding to buy your product? What will be their greatest motivator: New features? Unique benefits? Price? A special offer? Obviously, all of these can play a role, but the role for each is not the same from one advertiser to the next.

Consider the case of TurboTax software. Most prospects that aren't currently using TurboTax to prepare their tax return have never used tax preparation software before. Any spot promoting TurboTax needs to focus on features and benefits. Prospects need to know that TurboTax comes with IRS-approved forms, calculations are 100% guaranteed, it's updated every year to reflect the current tax codes, it's easy-to-use, and it has logic built right into it that will warn you about an entry that could trigger an audit.

While the price and offer in a TurboTax spot have to be attractive, the spot has a lot of heavy lifting to do in the area of overcoming potential obstacles to response. After all, tax software is still a relatively new product category, compared to life insurance, for example. And, to most consumers, tax preparation is a serious category. Just ask anyone who's ever been audited.

Now, compare the challenges of creating a spot for TurboTax with creating a spot for the magazine, *Sports Illustrated*. Is there anyone who doesn't know what *Sports Illustrated* is? Is there anyone who hasn't read a copy of it at one time or another? *Sports Illustrated* has been around for while. It has a lot of "pre-sold equity." Their television spots don't need to do much explaining about the product. In fact, we'd be willing to bet that a large percentage of sports fans in America have at one time or another subscribed to *Sports Illustrated* So, what does a spot need to do to motivate former subscribers to subscribe? Answer: Make them an incredible offer. And create a sense of urgency.

Bottom line: A *Sports Illustrated* spot is going to be much more *offer-driven* than a TurboTax spot. A TurboTax spot is going to be much more *product-focused* than a *Sports Illustrated* spot.

There's more to crafting a message strategy than product features and offers. Here's what Laura Huffman, Executive President of Matrix Direct, has to say: "Before you develop spots, it's important to assess whether you need to sell the prospect on the *need* for your product. If there is already widespread acceptance of the need, then your ad can focus on convincing the consumer that your particular product is the best *solution*. We sell life insurance, a mature category, so we've found that the most effective approach is not 'needs-based selling,' but rather 'solutions-based' selling. We don't feel compelled to spend time in our spots selling viewers on why they need life insurance."

For an example of "needs-based selling," just consider the case of ConsumerInfo.com, which is a credit report monitoring service that allows you to see what's in your credit report online instantly.

So, how do you go about selling something like this? You develop spots that educate the consumer on the need for your service like the FreeCreditReport.com spot in Figure 7.2. In this DMA Echo Award winning spot, a lovable, animated stick figure character learns that a surprise on his credit report could mean he'd be turned down for a mortgage, a car loan, even a credit card. Another spot in the campaign has a storyline designed to teach the stick figure and viewers that good credit is necessary not just to carry out all of life's big plans, but also to be ready to handle all of life's little surprises. The FreeCreditReport.com spots are excellent examples of "needs-based" selling.

Here's another example of an effective message strategy: A recent Proflowers.com spot opens with this line: "Just a friendly reminder . . . that Mother's Day is Sunday, May 11th. . . ." Why this opening? Because experience has shown that consumers order flowers within a two-week window leading up to a major holiday. And while everyone

Figure 7.2: Stick Figure, FreeCreditReport.com, The Response Shop, Inc.

	PRODUCT	FreeCreditReport.com	DATE	03/17/2002
	TITLE	Stick Figure	LENGTH	60
	AGENCY	The Response Shop		
	ADVERTISER	ConsumerInfo.com		

(MUSIC IN) FEMALE ANNCR: Psst! Do you have good credit?

STICK FIGURE: Uh-huh!

FEMALE ANNCR: Or do you only think you have?

STICK FIGURE: Hmmmm?

FEMALE ANNCR: Do you know how to check your credit report and find out?

STICK FIGURE: Uh-uh.

FEMALE ANNCR: A surprise on your credit report could mean you'd be turned down for a mortgage...

(SFX: SOUND OF ERASURE)

...a car loan...

(SFX: SOUND OF ERASURE)

...even a credit card

(SFX: SOUND OF ERASURE)

Which is why you should log onto FreeCreditReport.com.

At FreeCreditReport.com we'll show you how to find out online what's in your credit report...

...who's been checking it...

...and whether everything's accurate.

So log onto FreeCreditReport.com today or give us a call. You're going to do it now, aren't you?

STICK FIGURE: Mm-hm!

FEMALE ANNCR: Great! Now, how about you?

(SFX: FOOTSTEPS)
(MUSIC OUT)

Reprinted with permission of The Response Shop and FreecreditReport.com.

knows the dates of Christmas and Valentine's Day, Mother's Day lands on a different day every year. Hardly anybody in their target audience knows when Mother's Day is without Proflowers.com reminding them!

What's the point? Before you sit down to prepare a list of benefits to describe in your spot, first try to think like your prospect and figure out what they need to know to take action.

Television Tactics: Describe The Benefits

Another good exercise is to do some deep thinking about what you're really selling. And it's not always what you think. Take *Time-Life* Music, for example. What are they really selling? Music, right? Wrong. With some of their collections, they're selling memories.

"No matter what era we're talking about, whether we're talking about the Big Band era or the 1960s, our customers all say the same thing: They want to hear 'their' music again, the songs they listened to when they were young. Why? Because it takes them back to a wonderful time in their lives," says Mitch Peyser, VP of Marketing for *Time-Life* Music.

That's why, in many *Time-Life* Music spots, nostalgic footage is so important. Nothing will bring back memories of the sixties like a favorite song from that era, accompanied by authentic period footage.

One of *Time-Life's* spots for a Christmas collection features real holiday home movies supplied by *Time-Life* employees. The footage, from the early sixties, strikes a chord with its baby boomer audience. The spot opens with home movies of kids gleefully running down the stairs, toward the Christmas tree. It cuts to kids playing in the snow, and then it cuts to a boy sitting on his shiny new bike around the living room. The spot is full of charm. You'd have to be a robot to not feel a connection with that footage.

Of course, music and memories are just the beginning of the magic of these spots. The announcer v/o goes on to point out how many hours it would take to hunt down all of the individual songs included in the collection, if you could even find them.

Yup, *Time-Life's* done all the work for you, and delivered the original hits by the original artists in state-of-the-art digital sound. When the $26.99 price is finally revealed, the collection seems like a steal.

For another brilliant example of demonstrating benefits you only need to watch the Sharper Image Ionic Breeze infomercial. The Ionic Breeze is an air purifier. It takes pollutants, allergens, bacteria, pet dander, and other harmful particles out of the air. The marketing challenge: you can't actually see or hear the product working.

How do you demonstrate the benefit? Simple: You have the President of Sharper Image, Richard Thalheimer, wipe a damp sponge over the air filter and hold it up for the viewing audience to see. And what do they see: A sponge that is jet black with harmful pollutants that, if not for the Ionic Breeze, would be clinging to the inside of your lungs instead of that sponge.

By the time the viewer has finished watching the Sharper Image Ionic Breeze infomercial, they're completely convinced that they are not only buying an air purifier, but they're buying into a better way of living.

One more great example is a *Reader's Digest* Books spot from a few years ago that promoted their *Fix-It-Yourself Manual*. The spot opens with "Got a door that sticks? Don't call a carpenter, call a golfer! Because a golf tee here, under the hinge, will help a sticking door swing free." Not only is the opening question very engaging, but the Q&A format of the spot serves as a great device to demonstrate the types of practical solutions that the book delivers.

For another creative way to demonstrate benefits in a television spot, check out the flashback footage used in the TurboTax spot, entitled "Last Year."

The spot opens with a lovable on-camera male actor, speaking these lines: "It's tax time. But *I'm* not stressed. Because I've got TurboTax software! Not like *last* year . . . when I spent *hours* struggling with the forms, the manuals and the math!"

During the on-camera talent's not-so-happy walk down memory lane, the viewer is treated to humorous black and white footage of him struggling to prepare his tax return the year before. We then cut back to beautiful, color footage of him, contentedly working on his PC, as he looks to camera and says, confidently, "Well, not *this* year!"

Figure 7.3: Last Year, TurboTax.com, The Response Shop, Inc.

PRODUCT:	TURBOTAX	DATE:	01/01/03
TITLE:	LAST YEAR	LENGTH:	60
AGENCY:	THE RESPONSE SHOP		
ADVERTISER:	INTUIT		

7910 Ivanhoe Avenue, Suite 519
La Jolla, CA 92037
Phone: 858-456-6160

BERT: It's tax time. But *I'm* not stressed.

BERT: Because *this year*, I've got TurboTax Software!

BERT: Not like *last* year...

BERT: ... when I spent *hours* struggling with the forms...

BERT: ... the manuals...

ANNCR: ...and the *math*!

BERT: Well, not *this* year!
ANNCR: Presenting new Turbo Tax Deluxe - with the EasyStep Interview that asks you simple questions...

ANNCR: ...then puts your answers in all the right places with calculations guaranteed accurate.
BERT: It's so easy!

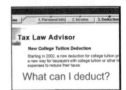

ANNCR: TurboTax Deluxe also points out deductions you might miss.
BERT: Like this one!

ANNCR: And includes IRS-approved forms! Simply print out your return, or file electronically to get your refund faster!

ANNCR: Call now, and try TurboTax Deluxe *free* for 30 days. If pleased, pay just $39.95.

ANNCR: So get TurboTax Deluxe *now*. For taxes made *easy*. And taxes done *right*.

The dramatized flashback is just one creative device available to television advertisers that is not available in other media. The spot is further enhanced by high-quality custom graphics and compelling screen shots. (To see this spot in its entirety, go to *www.response-lab.com*.)

A combination of live action footage and graphics can be very effective. One technique commonly used by music television marketers is the song and artist "crawl," which allows the advertiser to communicate most, if not all, of the repertoire included in the collection. This technique has been used by publishers, mortgage lenders, and insurance brokers to visually communicate long lists of features and benefits. Why do crawls work? Because they are very involving. Once someone starts to read, they keep reading. One more reason crawls work is because message comprehension and retention is always better when the message is communicated visually instead of aurally. (Reading is active, not passive!)

One advertiser, eHealthInsurance, Inc., used an "all text" spot that featured a word-for-word crawl of the announcer v/o copy. Every single word voiced by the announcer was included in the crawl. *Every single word.* In addition, key messages were highlighted with motion graphics to the right of the crawl. In the lower letterbox, the spot featured the URL: *www.eHealth.com*. The upper letterbox featured the words "Shop. Compare. Save." The upper and lower letterboxes stayed up nearly the entire length of the sixty-second spot. There was simply no way for anyone watching the spot to lose sight of the category and key consumer promise! Subtlety does not work on television.

On top of its heavy use of text and motion graphics, the eHealthInsurance announcer v/o copy was particularly benefit focused. Notice how often the words "you" and "your" are used in this excerpt from the spot:

Anncr: Just go to eHealth.com to get *instant* quotes from leading health insurance companies. So you can compare plans, prices and benefits side-by-side. Even apply online for the plan that's right for *you*. One that fits *your* budget, and *your* health needs!

The on-camera presenter is yet another format that is available to television advertisers that isn't available to print advertisers. When executed well, there is nothing more convincing than a presenter speaking to the camera. And on-camera presenters are promoting a lot more these days than juicers and vacuum cleaners. Consider this wonderful Christian Children's Fund spot:

Man, in a Brazilian Slum, Speaks to Camera   Look around you. Can you cure the world's poverty, hunger, lack of education and medical care . . . for 80 cents a day? Of course not. In this kind of poverty, what in the world *can* you do for 80 cents a day? Well, you can work *wonders*. Let's take *the 80-cent tour* with Brenna . . .

The presenter then goes on to show all of the great support that Christian Children's Fund provides to a needy child, including clean water, nourishing food, education, and medical care for just 80 cents a day.

Here's what Brian Gale, of Christian Children's Fund, had to say: "It's important that our spots communicate that a sponsor can truly make a difference in a child's life. We are an extremely efficient charity. In fiscal year 2004 over 80 percent of all funds raised were used for program services for children. Our spots work hard to communicate what the children get. We simply can't forget that it's truly *about the children*."

To drive the point home, Christian Children's Fund supers key messages like this one in its television spots: "One of America's most charitable charities—*Consumer's Digest*."

It's important to think through potential consumer objections, and address them in your spot. Here's how Unitrin Direct Auto Insurance addresses potential consumer objections in one of its spots:

On-Camera Presenter: But unlike those cut-rate companies, *you don't have to give up service.* In fact, you'll have your own team of dedicated professionals to answer your questions or handle your claims. *You don't have to give up security, either.* We're part of the top-rated Unitrin insurance family with over seventy years of experience and over five billion dollars in assets.

The Unitrin spot is also a great example of how one marketer turned key attributes, like seventy years of experience, into important consumer benefits, like security!

Television Tactics: Present The Offer

Remember the *Sports Illustrated* spot that we told you about earlier? The one that opens with the Dad interrogating his son about the magazines he's been hiding under the mattress? As the spot continues, it's revealed that the magazine the son cherishes is none other than *Sports Illustrated*. So, what is that the son feels he has to hide from Dad? He signed up for a trial subscription. After Dad hears the offer details, he decides he's going to get into the action and get a trial subscription, too! What a terrific way to hype the offer!

Sometimes the price is the offer. It can really pay off to put some creative thinking into how the price and value are expressed in a spot. Take this Matrix Direct television spot, as an example. It opens with this copy:

Anncr:	Fifty cents. It won't buy you a donut or a cup of coffee. But it could buy you $100,000 of term life insurance . . . .

The spot ends with this terrific call-to-action:

Anncr:	What can fifty cents a day do for *you?* To find out, call 1-800-222-5477.

Christian Children's Fund, an international child development agency based in Richmond, Virginia, provides more excellent examples of great price/value-driven offers. Here's an excerpt from one of their spots:

Spokesperson, to Camera:	What in this world does a child need to survive? Four things. Clean water to drink. Decent food to eat. A doctor when they need one. And a safe school to go to. And, sometimes, a fifth thing. *A sponsor*—to make the other four happen—with only 80 cents a day. Call Christian Children's Fund. We'll send a picture of a child like Ilene who needs four things, and *you*.

Here's another great call-to-action, from a Gevalia Kaffee spot. The spot promotes a continuity (negative option) coffee program. The product is not sold in stores, and the offer includes a special introductory price *and* premium to entice a customer into taking that first step. This type of direct response has been going on for years. Nothing new here, except for how brilliantly it's expressed:

Anncr:	"You won't find Gevalia on any corner. Yet it's within arm's reach. Simply call 1-800-957-1120 and we'll deliver two boxes of our exquisite coffee from Europe for just $10. You'll receive our coffee maker free, to ensure you taste Gevalia at its finest."
	Order now, and receive two free mugs. If you enjoy Gevalia, we'll send you more, automatically. The free coffee maker, free mugs and two boxes of freshly sealed Gevalia Kaffee, delivered to you with no further obligation. It's too delicious to let pass you by. Call 1-800-957-1120. If your passion is coffee, your pleasure would be Gevalia.

Wow! Television advertising has certainly come a long way since the early days. More and more, television is being used by traditional advertisers to acquire new customers, generate new leads, and support brands, including premium brands like America Online, Citibank, and Gevalia Kaffe. While fresh ideas are in evidence, the tried and-true direct response techniques that we've all relied on for years are still at the heart of it all.

Newsletters

Newsletters are a unique and interesting medium for a marketer to use. Today, with the advent and increased acceptance of online communication, e-newsletters have become one of the most viable ways to sustain conversation with people who have indicated interest in your products and/or services. Packed with information, they become valuable to their readers while simultaneously keeping a company's marketing message front and center. In fact, the information included in both online and print newsletters can become part of that company's branding. If a company gives me information that benefits me, I think highly of them and am therefore more inclined to continue our ongoing conversation and buy, subscribe, join, and so forth.

According to the Newsletter & Electronic Publishers Association (NEPA) *(www.newsletters.org)*, there are hundreds of thousands of newsletters in existence today. They can be grouped into three distinct categories: (1) subscription-based newsletters, (2) internal house organs, and (3) persuasive newsletters from organizations to customers and prospects. There are a number of online and print newsletter directories available. *The Oxbridge Directory of Newsletters* is one of the largest directories, listing more than fourteen thousand newsletters, bulletins, and fax letters.

Subscription-Based Newsletters

The dual purpose of a subscription-based newsletter is to educate its readers, i.e., sustain the conversation, and return a profit for the publisher. Consumer newsletters tend to be more general, covering topics such as health issues, financial investing, or travel. Business-to-business (B2B) newsletters often have a narrow focus, and if they are true to their mission, reporting is objective and the information covered cannot easily be found elsewhere. Editorial content can include primary research, surveys, interviews with leading experts, and industry trends. Because of these unique qualities, B2B newsletters can demand hefty subscription rates. The more exclusive and timely the information presented, the higher the price a subscriber will pay. Subscription-based newsletters can include marketing content: renewal forms, pass-along subscription forms, or advertising for related products and services.

Internal House Organs: Newsletters

Internal house organs or internal newsletters are usually created for the purpose of keeping employees informed about the activities and policies within an organization. They are generally used in larger companies, especially those with a sales force or branches located throughout the United States or around the world. Although their main purpose is to inform, internal newsletters are also used to increase loyalty and instill corporate values and goals.

A number of years ago, Liberty Mutual transferred several major divisions from Boston, Massachusetts, to Dover, New Hampshire. A new Executive Vice President (EVP) was hired, and although some employees moved from Boston to Dover, there were many new hires. The EVP had a progressive vision of how his divisions should operate. He created an ambitious set of goals and wanted to make certain that employees knew what these were and how everyone could work together to accomplish them.

MKE Enterprises, of North Reading, Massachusetts, was called in to start a quarterly in-house newsletter that focused on these goals and how they were being achieved. The newsletter was also used to highlight new products, review training programs, welcome new employees, and reward individuals and teams for jobs well done. Although the overall purpose was information sharing, there was a very clear message that the new corporate culture and procedures were beneficial for both customers and employees.

Persuasive Newsletters for Customers and Prospects

The third type of newsletter—and the one that performs most obviously like a marketing vehicle—is a persuasive newsletter created especially for an organization's customers and prospects. Persuasive newsletters are produced to increase sales and lifetime value from current customers and convince prospects that they should be doing business with your company. There are two types of persuasive newsletters—business-to-consumer (B2C) and business-to-business (B2B).

Who Needs a Persuasive Customer and Prospect Newsletter? A wide range of companies can benefit from a customer/prospect newsletter. In the B2C arena, newsletters can be used by start-up companies and smaller firms. They lose their usefulness and become cost-prohibitive, at least in print form, when the audience becomes so large that the main persuasive vehicles become print ads and broadcast. For instance, to date, neither Coke nor Pepsi have created a newsletter to reach their millions of customers. However, they could create an e-newsletter targeted to a specific segment of their marketing universe, teens, for example, and include interactive material like games, quizzes, coupons, and so forth. A newsletter like this would aim to start and continue a more personal conversation with buyers.

Banks, credit card companies, and financial services firms send their customers full or mini-newsletters to discuss the benefits of using the products or services of the firm. They also include financial trends, tips, and other helpful information. Often, these newsletters are included with bills or statements.

Hotels and inns can use newsletters to thank customers for their visit, remind them of the reasons they stayed at the hotel, and inform them of plans for the upcoming season.

In the B2B world, a newsletter can be a highly effective form of communication. It's the salesperson without the sales pressure. It can also contain additional information that the salesperson may not give the customer or prospect.

Goals of a Persuasive Newsletter How does the newsletter differ from other marketing vehicles? It does not follow the five-step formula outlined in Chapter One (Get Attention; Describe the Benefits; Present the Offer; Ask for the Order; and Repeat the Offer). Instead, its format is more like a mini-magazine with articles and case studies.

The primary goals of a persuasive newsletter are to:

- Increase sales
- Turn prospects into customers
- Increase customer lifetime value

Secondary goals can include some or all of the following:

- Promote brand awareness
- Differentiate your products or services from the competition
- Acquaint the readership with your company, its employees, history, growth, community service, etc.
- Perform a public service function with generic articles that relate to your products or services

The idea is to provide your customers' and prospects' insights into your company—your people, your products or services, and your way of doing business—so they will choose your firm over the competition and remain loyal.

Who Should Receive Your Newsletter? A persuasive newsletter should certainly be sent to your current customer base. It can also be sent to lapsed customers and to prospects.

A word of advice about sending your newsletter to prospects. A newsletter should never be the first or only communication that prospects receive from your firm. If they receive a newsletter without any previous communication, they are likely to ask, "Why is this firm sending this to me? I have no relationship with this company." A newsletter should be sent after the prospect has received, and ideally responded to, a #10 package, a telephone call, or some other direct marketing message.

The Tone of the Conversation: "Me Me" versus "You You"

If you keep in mind the primary goals we discussed above, then you will understand that though the newsletter is about your company, it must also relate to the customer or prospect. Rather than brag about your firm's accomplishments, focus on the benefits of doing business with your company.

For example, if your newsletter has a column that highlights an employee or a team of employees, don't talk about what Jim Smith does for your company. Describe his job in terms of how it benefits your customers.

Specific Newsletter Messages

The first issue of a newsletter should include a "Welcome" from the President or CEO of the firm, explaining briefly why the newsletter is being sent to the recipient, what kind of information it will contain, and how it will benefit the reader. A smart technique is to end the Welcome with a "call to action," inviting readers to e-mail or fax their questions, comments, or article suggestions. Although customers may respond, don't expect to be deluged with suggestions. However, the request for input does indicate your concern for your readership and a desire to include them in the creative process.

In subsequent issues, the President's Message can highlight important topics and contain special messages. Any major company announcement, expansion, mergers, and so forth, should be part of the President's Message, and can be expanded upon elsewhere in the newsletter.

The cover article should have genuine news value. It can discuss a major company announcement, highlight new products or senior management additions. A financial services newsletter can talk about topics that are valuable to the reader, such as the importance of estate planning, trusts, and annuities.

A pharmaceutical company newsletter to business customers and prospects might talk about urgent issues in the healthcare field, trends, customer concerns, profitability, new legislation, and new products. A newsletter to consumers from the same company would talk about health issues surrounding the condition treated by the products that the firm produces. There are strict regulations concerning publishing legal, financial, or health-related advice, and your corporate attorneys should be consulted.

Other articles can include tips, industry news, calendar of events, and information on the products and services your company offers. The list is endless. In planning an outline of your topics, always ask yourself—will this interest or benefit my readers?

Newsletters can also be beneficial for non-profits. They can be used as a major vehicle to inform supporters how their donations are being spent, describe activities of the non-profit, and persuade donors to give again. The newsletter can also be sent to lapsed donors in an effort to reactivate them.

A number of the food banks around the country send out newsletters a few times a year with their fundraising appeals. They explain how food pantries and shelters use the food they obtain from the food banks, and how thousands of lives are changed for the better. They also use newsletters to thank food donors and sponsors, and recognize volunteer efforts.

Real life stories and mini-case studies are more convincing than any fiction you can create. They bring the reader into the lives of the people you are serving and dramatically demonstrate how donations are helping. Real life stories are an especially useful tool in fundraising newsletters.

Case studies and testimonials can be used in B2B newsletters as well. They can describe innovative ways that clients are using your products, how they are saving time or money with your products, and how you work with clients to solve their problems.

What Messages Should Not Be Conveyed in a Newsletter?

Unless your organization is small and your customers are like family, you should not include articles about Joe's son, who won a bike race or Mary, who just had a baby. If your customers don't know Joe and Mary, the information, although sweet, is irrelevant.

If your firm is in the midst of, or has just weathered a crisis, should you address it in the newsletter? This question is hard to answer and depends largely on individual circumstances. In general, if the crisis was just a "blip" on the radar screen in terms of how it affected your customers, a newsletter probably is not the best way to deal with it. However, if it did affect your customers, and was solved, then it may be positive to tell customers about the problem and how it was handled.

How Often? What Size? Two-Color or Four-Color?

Newsletters can be sent out whenever you have news for your customers and prospects. Generally, however, they are sent out four to six times a year. Twice per year is better than not at all, but two issues sent six months apart lack continuity. More than six mailings a year is probably too many, unless you are talking about e-mail newsletters, which we will discuss later on in this chapter.

A printed newsletter can range from a simple, two-sided, single sheet or four pages (11″ × 17″ folded) to as many pages as you want. Every issue does not have to be the same size. You can produce a four-pager when there is not much news, and increase to a six or eight pager if there are more topics you want to cover. One newsletter for a dietitians' trade association varied throughout the year from twenty to thirty-six pages, but that is an exception. Remember, many people don't sit down for hours and read, so generally it is recommended to keep a printed newsletter to eight pages or less.

Whether you publish in black and white, two-, or four-color depends upon two things, 1.) your budget, and 2.) the products or services you are trying to sell. If you are selling clothing, travel, or food where four-color is an integral part of the sell, then by all means spend the extra dollars and go with four-color. If you are a non-profit that wants to show your donor base that you are conserving resources, or if your product or service does not need glamour shots, we recommend working with two-color. The exception to this is if you have a short print run and can use digital printing, then the cost difference can be inconsequential, so it may be a good idea to use four-color.

The Writing, Photography, and Design Processes

Should a newsletter be produced in-house or should it be outsourced? There is no right or wrong answer to this question. The only definite advice we can give you is that it should not be an after-thought, given to an assistant who already has a "full plate." Producing a high quality, well-written newsletter is time-consuming, and takes the skills of both a writer and a designer.

The main advantage of producing an in-house newsletter is that costs, generally, will be lower. The key benefit of outsourcing the newsletter is that you can use experts with considerable experience in producing newsletters. They will look at your company from an outsider's perspective and may have a better view of the topics that will interest your readers.

Whether your newsletter is produced in-house or outsourced, your initial step is to determine your target audience and to agree on the overall image of the publication. Next, you should establish the frequency of publication, the number of pages, and whether it will be a two- or four-color newsletter.

"When we create a newsletter for a client," said Marilyn Ewer, President of MKE Enterprises, "we talk to the individuals involved to develop goals, a clear editorial focus, and an image. We then develop an initial list of twenty to thirty newsletter names that we give to the client. The client pares the list down to three or four, and then makes a final choice. Once the name is chosen, we can then create the masthead and overall design. This design is an integral part of the message."

Your newsletter should always be easy to read. If your audience tends to be older, consider a slightly larger type size. If your company is a leader in the industry, growing and aggressive, you should opt for a clean, contemporary look. If you are celebrating 100 years in business or are a cozy bed and breakfast in Maine, you may want a more traditional look and feel. Image can change dramatically by varying typestyle and design.

It is important to allow enough time to create an image that suits your firm. Once the name and look are established, you really want to maintain them to achieve continuity. Subsequent issues will use the design template with adjustments for article length and topics.

While you are working on the overall design, you can also develop an editorial outline for the first issue. If the newsletter is being produced by an outside firm, there should be one internal "point person" who has overall newsletter content/production responsibility. The point person should choose at least one employee who is the expert for each editorial topic. Then, the newsletter writer should interview these employees to gain information for the articles. This procedure maximizes the internal involvement of the organization. Interviews can be done in person or over the phone.

Do not ask individuals within the company to write their own articles. When this occurs, article quality varies greatly, and often, an engineer, scientist, or salesperson will spend an inordinate amount of time producing an article that is not really usable. This can lead to frustration and wounded egos.

If an individual is not comfortable being interviewed, you can ask if a list of questions sent ahead of the interview would help. This often puts the person at ease, because he or she can prepare answers. If this technique does not work, you can ask the person to jot down, in outline style, major points to be covered with details, and this can be turned into an article. Most people, however, have no trouble being interviewed.

Once a first draft is written, it is sent to the in-house point person. Generally, he or she will make edits and circulate it to the individuals who have been interviewed, so that they can make comments, too. If articles involve people from client companies, they too should be part of the approval process. And if there is any company-sensitive or financial/legal information, make sure to include the corporate attorneys early in the approval process

Usually a newsletter goes through two drafts to a final version. If the newsletter is written internally, the point person may be the writer or be responsible for designating a writer.

Photos, charts, illustrations, and graphs add information and visual interest—they should be an integral part of every newsletter. Unless they are large four-color photos, graphics do not add greatly to the cost of production. Since readers usually look at photos first, be sure each photo has a caption.

The Newsletter Business Reply Device

Newsletters can and should include a business reply card (BRC). The BRC should offer more information on your products or services, white papers on key topics, or other options tailored to your business goals.

Integrating Newsletters with Other Marketing Campaigns

As mentioned previously, newsletters should not be the only marketing effort. They can be a powerful complement, and should be integrated into a larger marketing campaign.

Producing an Online HTML or All-Text Newsletter

You can produce an online newsletter in either HyperText Mark-Up Language, commonly known as HTML, or in text. HTML uses "tags" to read the structure of hypertext documents, including copy and graphics. Text, as the term implies, refers to the use of text only.

Although the reasons for communications are the same, the format of an online newsletter is very different from a print newsletter. The key difference is that many recipients will not print it out, so they will be reading it on the screen.

Most people do not like to read long blocks of copy on screen, so all articles should be short, with headlines, usually in a different typeface, to break the copy visually. Paragraph widths should be fairly narrow, to fit within the screen size.

One online technique that is gaining popularity is to start or summarize the article in the newsletter and give a link to the reader to access the complete story. If you choose to organize your newsletter this way, be sure to write summaries that are compelling enough to motivate your readers to click through.

As mentioned previously, in print newsletters, photos are important. In online newsletters, photos add considerably to the size of the file, and unless you know that all your readers have high-speed connections, it is advisable to keep photos to a minimum, and make sure they are low resolution and small in size.

Although the interviewing and writing processes are the same as for a print newsletter, the design and production processes are different. Once they are written, HTML and all-text newsletters can be produced and e-mailed within a few days since they do not need to be printed and mailed. They can be less expensive to produce, compared to a print newsletter.

The concise format, along with shorter production schedules enable online newsletters to be more timely. Many organizations and trade associations use online newsletters to publicize events such as upcoming meetings.

Another key difference between print and online newsletters is the pass-along factor. Although a print newsletter is often passed around, once it leaves a person's possession, it can no longer be used for reference. With an online newsletter, a reader can easily forward it to others, yet still retain the original.

The reply process with an online newsletter can be instantaneous. Readers can choose the reply option from their e-mail software and comment on an article, register for an event, answer a survey, or request more information about a product or service.

HTML newsletters can contain banner ads and color graphics. Most companies producing online newsletters are using this format, but produce all-text versions too. In fact, some service bureaus insist that the newsletter publisher provide both versions. Newer versions of e-mail software can receive HTML newsletters; old versions still have trouble with them. E-mail software is rapidly improving, and problems with HTML and file size are fast disappearing.

The Dirty Secret of Publishing an Effective E-newsletter: The Nitty-Gritty Details

By Debbie Weil
Publisher, WordBiz Report

You've decided to build a relationship with prospects and customers by creating an e-mail newsletter. It's part of your larger marketing communications strategy: initiating and continuing a conversation with your target audience.

How do you launch and sustain an e-newsletter with enough flair and substance to fulfill your business objectives—namely, more leads, increased sales, and heightened credibility for your company?

Whether you're doing it to generate leads or make a profit, you must have a formula for publishing issue after issue.

You're in trouble if you don't. You may find yourself running out of steam after a few months. What to write about next? Or maybe your newsletter fails to develop a distinctive identity. It has a few articles or tidbits of information in it, but readers are not sure what to expect. And they stop opening it.

Here is the dirty secret of publishing an e-newsletter: the nitty-gritty details.

Is killer content killing you?

Too much of it? Not enough? Do you notice the months getting shorter and your deadlines rolling around with increasing frequency?

If publishing a regular e-mail newsletter is a daunting prospect—or has become a chore—listen up for seven nitty-gritty tips from the trenches. (Tips are written specifically for HTML newsletters.)

1. RE-EXAMINE WHY YOU ARE PUBLISHING

If you've published for a while (say, at least four issues), you've established a track record with your readers. But what are you getting in return?

Most e-newsletters are a cross between a branding tool and a lead-generating tactic. Evaluate which yours is. And which marketing tactic is more important to you right now. If you're not generating a significant number of leads with each issue, you might consider cutting back to bi-monthly (every two months) or even quarterly.

You'll get more ROI out of your e-newsletter if you continue to publish it, rather than run out of steam after four or five issues.

2. ASSIGN A POINT PERSON

Designate an inside point person to keep track of all the details. Whether or not you are using a web-based service to deliver your e-newsletter, you need at least one staff member whose job responsibility includes "getting the newsletter out."

This can be a junior staffer who is meticulous as well as a good writer and editor. Ideally, he or she will have a basic knowledge of HTML. Be nice to this person.

3. TAKE STOCK OF YOUR EDITORIAL RESOURCES

Do you have a CEO who's got a real touch when it comes to writing? His or her informal musings about hot topics in your industry—or a personal note—can create the "voice" of your newsletter.

On the other hand, if no one in your group has the ability to write clearly, informally and succinctly (key to successful online content), outsource. Hire an outside editor and feed him or her article ideas on an ongoing basis. As marketing consultant Sandy Thorpe puts it, "Many businesses avoid newsletters because of the perceived time sink. And that is indeed the case if you're trying to do it all in-house by employees who have other priorities."

4. PLANNING YOUR NEXT ISSUE

The best time to plan the content of your next issue is immediately after sending out the current one. You're "in the groove," so to speak, and able to think most clearly about your publication.

Within hours of hitting Send you'll know what attracted the most interest from your readers—and whether your subject line inspired a click to open the issue.

This is where your content formula comes into play. Ideally, you have a formula for a mix of articles, topics, departments, letter from the CEO, quizzes, etc. Be prepared to change it.

If click-through reporting tells you that the number two article is the most popular, analyze why. Make that the lead next time. If you ask for reader feedback on a certain topic and get a flood of responses, you have the basis for an article in the next issue.

5. CALENDARIZE THE PROCESS

OK, that's a dreadful word. But it's easy to let the weeks go by and realize that your next issue is "due out" next week. Before panic sets in, turn to your point person and ask him or her to come up with a publishing calendar. Or hand the task to an outside editor. This should include deadline dates for:

- —collecting article ideas
- —getting reprint permission, if necessary
- —turning ideas into rough drafts
- —dropping the copy into your HTML template with placeholder titles
- —editing and cutting within the HTML (the copy is almost always too long)
- —writing final article titles and a draft subject line
- —sending test issues to your internal "newsletter approval" group
- —checking every link
- —printing out to do a final proof for typos
- —sharpening the subject line one last time before you publish (yes, do this last; it's key!)

You'll note that a number of the tasks above are not dissimilar to what your web team does before revising your home page and reposting it.

6. KEEP AN IDEA FILE FOR EACH ISSUE

The best time to plan future issues of your newsletter (other than right after sending) is when you're not thinking about your newsletter at all. You may be responding to e-mail, looking for information on the web, speaking to a colleague on the phone, etc.

If a URL on another site sparks an idea, immediately cut and paste it into a "running ideas" file on your hard drive. If it's an e-mail from a potential contributor, do the same. Better yet, put ideas into folders named April '05 or May '05. If you've got a shared drive, your point person will have access to them as well.

If it's a magazine or newspaper article, tear it out and stick it into a paper folder labeled by month of publication.

7. APPLY THE NEWSWORTHY TEST THE DAY BEFORE PUBLISHING

Finally, apply the newsworthy test. Has something come up that will be of keen interest to your readers? A new regulation, a connection to world events? If so, add a blurb in your CEO or publisher's note to reflect this. Making your newsletter "newsworthy" adds huge credibility.

And if the point is to establish your company or organization as knowledgeable and an industry leader, you're a step closer to a solid ROI for all your efforts.

Useful Links:

TOP 10 TIPS TO LAUNCH AN E-NEWSLETTER PLUS
FIVE TIPS TO GET IT OPENED

A succinct but meaty guide you can print out and use immediately as a starting point to launch or improve your e-mail newsletter. Available as a PDF e-book at: *www.wordbizstore.com*

HOW TO GET YOUR E-NEWSLETTER READ: FROM THE
NITTY-GRITTY TO CONTENT THAT CREATES CUSTOMERS

Complete edited transcript of the first annual WordBiz E-newsletter Seminar, including PowerPoint slides, worksheets and articles plus bonus tips and resources.

Available both as a printed report (100 + pages) and as a PDF e-book at: *www.wordbizstore.com*

About Debbie Weil

Debbie is an e-newsletter expert and publisher of *WordBiz Report*, winner of The Newsletter on Newsletter's Gold Award for Online Subscription Newsletter as well as an APEX Award for Publication Excellence. Subscribe free at *www.wordbiz.com/signup.html.*

To Learn More

- Browse the WordBiz Store at *www.wordbizstore.com*
- Read Debbie's blog at: *www.debbieweil.com*

- More about Debbie at: *www.wordbiz.com/resume.html*
- Latest issue of WordBiz Report at: *www.wordbizreport.com*
    dweil@wordbiz.com
    www.wordbiz.com
    tel: + 1 202.364.5705
    fax: + 1 202.686.4746

Mini-Case Study—The Forest Hills Newsletter

The Forest Hills Newsletter was chosen for this mini-case study because of its unique focus, as well as the challenges and opportunities that it presented.

The Forest Hills Cemetery, located in Boston, Massachusetts, is one of the premier rural garden cemeteries in America. Founded in 1848, it is the final resting place for famous military, literary, and historic figures such as William Lloyd Garrison, Anne Sexton, and Eugene O'Neill. It also has outstanding sculpture, beautiful gardens, and hosts many events that are attended by area residents.

As part of an overall marketing plan that includes direct mail campaigns, agency GHW Associates of Mansfield, Massachusetts asked MKE Enterprises to create a newsletter for the cemetery.

The immediate challenge was that the cemetery already had a newsletter, *The Forest Hills Flame*, which focused on the historic and artistic significance of the cemetery. Because the cemetery still has land available for gravesite development, this new newsletter needed to focus narrowly on "selling the cemetery."

MKE Enterprises proposed a wide range of names, and the client selected *The Forest Hills Newsletter*. The audience for this new newsletter comprised families who have loved ones buried in the cemetery; individuals who have had loved ones cremated at Forest Hills; those who have preplanned for their final resting place; individuals who have responded to previous direct mail efforts; and funeral directors, who are often asked to recommend a cemetery.

Death, burial, and cremation are not easy topics to write about. The first issue had a "Welcome" from the President, articles such as "Planning Ahead Offers Benefits for You and Your Loved Ones," and a description of the new "Chapel of Light." Topics in other issues included "The Grieving Process—Everyone Experiences Loss and Sorrow Differently," and an overview of new areas of the cemetery being developed.

Production was relatively simple, four pages (11" × 17"), two-color, folded in thirds, and mailed in a #10 envelope. The first issue was mailed with a cover letter from the President describing the newsletter and explaining why it was being sent to the recipient. A Business Reply Card (BRC) offering more information on various topics was included with this, as well as subsequent issues.

The newsletter has been well received and response has been very positive. Even though this newsletter is not a "pure" marketing vehicle, BRC returns have generated an almost 2.5% response rate.

E-mail

When e-mail first arrived on the scene, we approached it with great excitement. Here, at last, was a medium exquisitely designed to take advantage of direct or one-to-one marketing's primary conversational goals: personalized message, speed and convenience of response, and low-cost implementation. E-mail loomed as—and remains—a marketer's ideal testing ground. Different offers and creative concepts can be tried out with little or no expense. Unlike traditional snail mail, e-mail tests carry no postage, printing, or fulfillment costs, which can often be substantial enough to deter testing at all.

An e-mail communication offered a marketer's dream environment. Reading an e-mail on the screen is an even more intimate experience than reading a piece of mail. Your reader is enmeshed in the online experience and captive to your message once they've clicked through to open your e-mail. And there's the rub. What happened from the time AOL and Delphi first made e-mail generally accessible online in 1993 (although Compuserve had been using it successfully before then) is that the number of e-mails being sent grew exponentially, and that rate shows no sign of stopping. According to International Data Corporation, "The number of worldwide e-mail mailboxes is expected to increase at a 138% growth rate, from 505 million in 2000 to 1.2 billion in 2005."

More pertinent from our prospect/customer's perspective is that according to Jupiter Research, "between e-mail marketing messages, personal communications, spam, and junk mail" the average e-mail user will receive about 3,800 e-mails each year." That's a lot of mail to go through.

Just as traditional direct mail, or snail mail, attracted detractors even as it helped boost business profits, now e-mail has attracted perhaps an even larger or at least more vocal cadre of opponents. Receiving e-mail at work or at home is no longer a new or unique experience for most people. If you're like most of us, you're now met with an onslaught of correspondence, some of which is urgent, some of which is personal, and much of it unwanted.

So, just as traditional direct mailers had to learn how to make their outer envelopes stand out from the crowd of envelopes surrounding them in a recipient's mailbox, now e-mailers face the same daunting challenge.

How does *my* e-mailed marketing message stand out from scores of others? How does *my* e-mailed correspondence survive that one-second decision on the part of the recipient whether or not to click delete? Some companies have figured out the answer. The Direct Marketing Association reports that two-thirds of all companies surveyed showed increased sales in 2001 as a result of using e-mail marketing. The use of e-mail as a marketing medium shows no sign of disappearing.

What remains promising about e-mail as a marketing conversation medium is the concept of permission-based, or opt-in e-mail. In truth, the Internet itself is permission-based since the reader/user is always in control of turning their computer on or off, and clicking here or there.

Opting-In to the Conversation

Once someone opts-in to receive your marketing communications, they've given a green light to a conversation. Remember that party we talked about in Chapter One, where you're standing next to attractive, interesting people? Well, someone who's opted-in to receive your e-mails is someone who smiles, nods, and encourages you to talk more with them. In this way, opt-in e-mail marketing—developed from either outside lists or house lists—is a marketing conversation that really starts off on the right foot.

In *The Engaged Customer*, Hans Peter Brondmo explains how e-mail acquisition programs are like a series of dates. "Once you decide you want to start going out, you have to figure out how you're going to meet people." Will it be through opt-in, such as "Click here to sign up for our FREE newsletter;" double opt-in, where a secondary communication arrives asking someone to confirm their decision to opt-in, either by responding to an e-mail or linking to a web page; or opt-out, as in the following examples:

> You are receiving this item as a registered member of 6Figure-Jobs.com. If you no longer wish to receive 6FigureNews for the Executive, please follow the prompt at the end of this e-mail. *http://www.6FigureJobs.com*

> To unsubscribe to this message, please click on: mailto: **unsubscribe@alight.com** or copy and paste this address into your e-mail "TO" field and then send the e-mail message to us.

> If you do not wish to receive e-mail from us, please change your mailing preferences at: **https://www.learningannex.com/secure/pref.taf?uid = 189692**

Ironically, many online marketers offer easily accessible "opt-out" or "unsubscribe" options in an attempt to reassure would-be subscribers.

Integrating E-mail and Other Media

While some companies use e-mail to refer their customers to other, non-competitive companies, others direct their leads to partner programs. The most obvious examples are airline web sites like United and American Airlines. On the web site AA.com, customers may encounter various ads from restaurants to car rental companies, many of which are partners in AAdvantage Partners and Mileage Programs. E-mails from AA.com may refer recipients to these programs that include ways to earn and use miles through hotels, financial service or telecommunications providers, retail shops and sites, and even charities. One listing on AA.com explains AAdvantage members have already donated more than $3 million dollars to the National Park Foundation, for which they've earned millions of bonus miles. By donating $10 or more to America's Proud Partner campaign, an individual can earn 10 bonus miles for every $1 given. Such a donation can be given through a special landing page or by calling an 800-number—a fine example of a multi-media conversation that benefits all parties involved!

Another great implementer of e-mail conversations is amazon.com. They've set a standard for recognition of previous customer purchases and interests, and they use the information they've gathered to great, response-generating effect by sending e-mails that recommend similar books or other products.

Sometimes, conversations have long lag times. You may not see a childhood or college friend for several years, and then when you meet, you both pick up the conversation as though it's never ended. Hickory Farms provides a good example of this when each holiday season, they send customers an e-mail listing the previous year's gift purchases for out-of-town friends and relatives. The form arrives filled out; the transaction couldn't be easier for busy holiday shoppers.

Speed, convenience, and personalization: remember the promises e-mail held out before us marketers? Now it seems that everybody is online exchanging e-mail, instant messages, jokes, and good-luck chain mails with friends and colleagues. Marketers are right there with them, sending one-time promotional offers, posting e-newsletters and e-magazines, reminding users to renew memberships to professional organizations, and offering online specials to customers buying everything from shampoo to flowering shrubs to kayaks to dog food.

It's easy to see why emarketing is sometimes called the golden child of the twenty-first century. And why not? E-mail marketing is cheap, easy, and effective. The numbers prove it. According to GartnerG2 Research, e-mail costs range from five to seven dollars per thousand while direct mail costs range from $500 to $700 per thousand.

In addition, a recent PricewaterhouseCoopers survey found that a vast majority (83%) of Internet users go online *primarily to use their e-mail*. So, if you want to reach Internet users, e-mail seems a logical way to go. Still, no discussion of e-mail marketing is complete without examining the phenomenon that's causing the greatest controversy on the e-mail marketing frontier: SPAM.

Spam

According to a Pew survey conducted in June 2004, about a third of e-mail users said spam made their time online annoying or unpleasant—this despite a new federal anti-spam law put into effect January 2004. This CAN SPAM law, as it is known, requires that unsolicited e-mail include both valid e-mail and snail mail addresses, an opt-out option for recipients, and self-identification as unsolicited. Since its passage, the law has led to hundreds of lawsuits against spammers.

It has become common knowledge that unsolicited e-mail has lower open and click-through rates than opt-in e-mail. So it's no surprise that when Clickz.com columnist Heidi Anderson posted a query from a reader who wanted to increase his web site sales by sending out "champagne spam . . . brief, tasteful mailings," she was deluged with negative comments. Anderson summed up the responses as, "Spam Equals Brand Suicide."

Overwhelmingly, individual marketers and formal studies agree that consumers are annoyed by spam from well-known companies, and even more annoyed by spam from unknowns. High-class Spam? Forget it! Emarketers might keep in mind this sobering statistic from Iconocast: "Thirty-six percent of experienced online users use fake e-mail addresses when registering at sites to avoid spam."

Marketing columnist Jeanne Jennings was overwhelmed with similar reader responses echoing industry-wide concerns about spam. Capstone Communications Group's Keith Thirgood thought unsolicited emessaging could "destroy e-mail as a medium of communication." Michelle Stute from OCjobSite.com wrote that, "Spam is bad PR, and any business that cares about its image and its product will shun it."

Of course, online lists are sometimes shared. Here's a representative message from PostMasterDirect.com, which forwards information to subscribers to internet.com, a marketing information web site:

> Thank you for your opt-in e-mail confirmation! Welcome to our free service! We strive to bring useful information direct to your e-mail box without spamming, and without compromising your privacy! We do not sell our lists, but we mail on behalf of

vendors who want to contact you with interesting news and product information in the topics you have specified.

Still, despite the challenges spam poses to our industry consider that, according to eMarketer, "Eighty percent of e-mail marketing messages elicit responses within forty-eight hours to a week, versus six to eight weeks for a traditional direct mail piece."

The abuse of public trust caused by illegal spammers and dangerous viruses and worms has been severe, but it is important to recognize that e-mail is and will probably remain a valid, effective, and profitable means of marketing. Even Lee Rainie, director of the Pew Foundation's study, acknowledged that "The reality of the situation is that e-mail is embedded in most people's lives."

Viral Marketing

Viral marketing, is a term used to identify word-of-mouth marketing, or what Brondmo identifies as "word of mouse." You're probably already familiar with the ways direct mail can be used in member-get-a-member programs, such as when the Direct Marketing Association of Washington offers a discounted dues structure to any existing member who recruits a new member for DMAW. Such programs exist on the Internet as well, sometimes formally and sometimes not.

When customers receive an e-mail they find particularly valuable, they often forward it to friends, family, and business associates. The result is some free advertising for the product or service. In addition, e-mails forwarded by personal acquaintances are far more likely to be read. Many marketing programs are able to track even forwarded messages, which obviously reach a naturally-targeted customer base. It's becoming common practice to reward customers who forward messages with perks like discounts, contests or sweepstakes entries, or special information, e.g., white papers or insider tips. It's wise for the e-mail marketer to consider adding creative elements that help spread their message, such as a pass-along notice on an e-mail, similar to the pass-along response forms in traditional mailings. These can multiply results substantially.

Women in particular are aware of how quickly petitions against breast cancer, for example, have spread among friends on the web. And they're often eager to share important news about their health, their children, and the world with friends. One organization which demonstrated the fast and effective ability of women to spread the word is the Million Mom March. In 2000, MOM rallied 700,000 women in Washington, D.C. to demand stricter gun laws. Now, they're planning a second march in DC on Mother's Day 2004. On their web site, there's a link to www.MoveOn.org. A nonprofit grass-roots organization, MoveOn began with a distinct goal: namely, to empower politically marginalized citizens with a political voice. In 1998, MoveOn began with an online petition that called upon citizens to voice their opinions and concerns about the impeachment trial of President Clinton. Through MoveOn, citizens rebelled against the very idea of an impeachment trial, calling it a waste of time, and lobbied for the nation to "move on" to more pressing issues. More recently, MoveOn has helped spread the word about ending the war in Iraq and protested California's recall elections. With more than 1,700,000 online activists, MoveOn is a great example of the sheer power and influence of viral marketing. Additionally, politicians, both liberal and conservative, have found viral marketing to be quite rewarding. Howard Dean used the Internet to raise funds for and spread the word about his campaign for the 2004 Democratic presidential nomination. Conservative factions have also discovered the benefits of viral marketing: Ralph Reed and the Christian Coalition have used viral marketing techniques to successfully spread awareness about their concerns.

Creating an E-mail Campaign

Let's get started on our own ecampaign. As in any marketing effort, the first step is to make sure consumers read our message. And before we can take that first step, we have to decide how to offer the message.

Formats Since one-half of all U.S. home Internet users have some sort of filtering solution in place, according to a new *Arbitron* and *Edison Media Research* report, it's critical for any e-mail marketer to carefully consider their choices in format. While rich, or streaming media (now often called interactive broadcasting) may appeal creatively to e-mail marketers, it may or may not make its full impact on its intended recipient.

Formats that can be used to create an ecampaign include:

- *HTML* (HyperText Markup Language) is the formatting used to create web pages: a combination of text and images in rich colors.
- *Text* messages are just that: the printed word, with no graphics; your basic form of personal e-mails.
- *Streaming Media* is perhaps closest to online mini-movies: combining audio and visual, it utilizes text and graphics, moving images, sound tracks and special effects.

The creative elements you choose may appear differently—or not at all—according to the recipient's e-mail client, browser, security settings, patches, updates, and more. For instance, while there's been a great deal of interest recently in adding Flash to e-mail, most e-mail HTML browsers simply aren't equipped to handle it. You need to predict your prospect or customer's receipt of your advertising message. So don't use any of the exciting formatting options available for e-mail unless you're absolutely certain your recipient wants and can view them.

The debate of HTML vs. plain text e-mails is an ongoing one, but keep in mind that a 2003 survey by Lucent Marketing indicated that more than half of AOL users preferred plain text. Even more important, the survey showed plain text e-mails were more effective, out pulling HTML messages during three months of testing—sometimes by as much as 100%!

E-mail Roadblocks

As with any media you use for your campaign, your marketing message must be direct, personal, and clear. Additionally, emarketers must avoid setting up roadblocks to potential customers. Roadblocks are any procedures that make it more difficult for consumers to open or read your emessages.

Sender Lines and Subject Lines The best e-mail is e-mail that gets read. Each message you send should offer clear, recognizable sender addresses and subject lines so consumers know whether they're about to open a message from L.L. Bean touting the latest backpacking tent or a message from Barnes & Noble touting their latest best-seller.

The first thing your customer sees on opening their e-mailbox is your sender identification (or return address) and the subject line. Here are some sample sender lines:

> *shop@nordstrom* An easily identifiable retailer, with a call to action built right in.

> *White_Flower_Fa* The name of this fairly well-known catalog company is truncated but still identifiable as White Flower Farm.

> *cmprn123652@gm20* This return address is incomprehensible and unlikely to be opened.

> *editor-8276@cancun.stationsnetwork.com* This return address for a company selling free computer training gets shortened to editor-8276@canc when it reaches America Online mailboxes. You'll want to check all of your creative to see how it translates on various platforms.

According to the July 2, 2003 issue of *DM News*, opt-in recipients who open their e-mail messages from Churchhill Downs and other racetracks and betting parlors are 16% more likely to make return visits. ExactTarget Connect's e-mail software sends out regular e-newsletters and e-mails like these:

Figure 9.1: Sample E-mail and E-newsletter

-----Original Message-----

From: Twin Spires Club [mailto:mailinglist@kyderby.com]

Sent: Thursday, June 05, 2003 4:03 PM

To: customer

Subject: Mark, Win 100,000 Twin Spires Club Points!

See if Funny Cide will be the first Triple Crown Winner since

Affirmed in 1978!

WIN 100,000 TSC POINTS--

Reprinted with permission of Churchill Downs Incorporated.

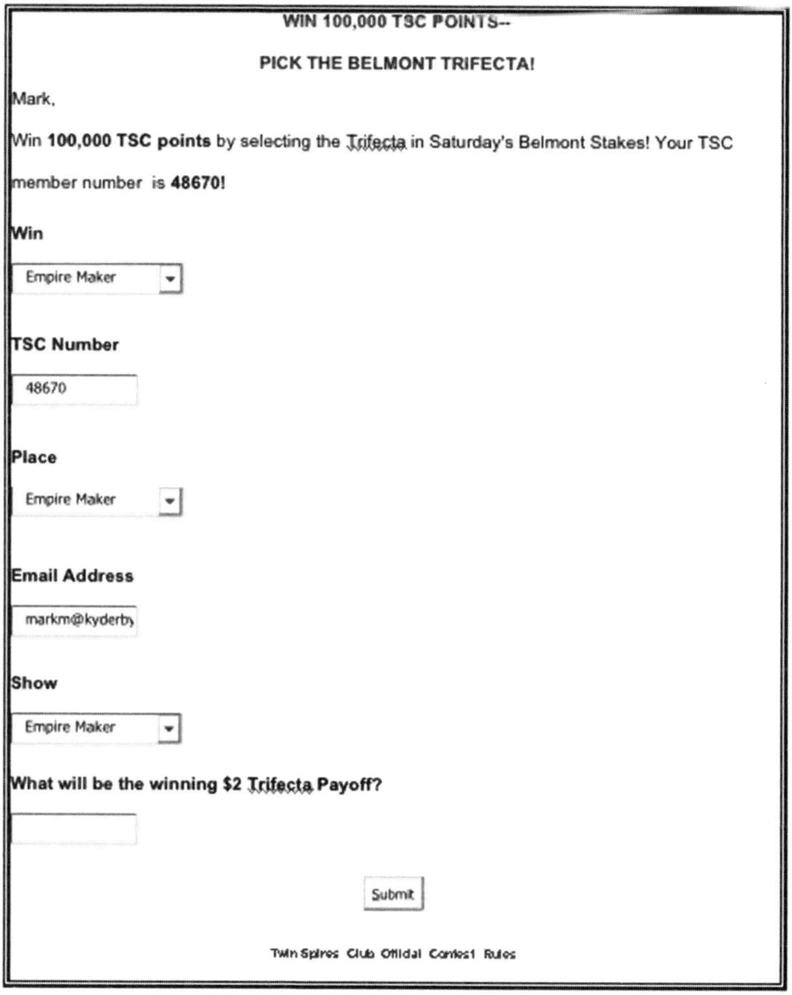

WIN 100,000 TSC POINTS--

PICK THE BELMONT TRIFECTA!

Mark,

Win **100,000 TSC points** by selecting the Trifecta in Saturday's Belmont Stakes! Your TSC member number is **48670!**

Win

| Empire Maker ▼ |

TSC Number

| 48670 |

Place

| Empire Maker ▼ |

Email Address

| markm@kyderby |

Show

| Empire Maker ▼ |

What will be the winning $2 Trifecta Payoff?

| |

Submit

Twin Spires Club Official Contest Rules

Reprinted with permission of Churchill Downs Incorporated.

Belmont Stakes DRF Free Online PP's!

Get **FREE** PP's, **FREE** DRF analysis, or purchase full card DRF Past Performances.

Check out the Twin Spires Club Auction today!

Bid on all these great items with your Twin Spires Club points!

It's easy! Just register at the Twin Spires Club auction website in order to buy auction items. You will receive a password and you can begin to place your bids on great racing memorabilia.

Items currently up for bid include:

Affirmed Bobblehead

Autographed 1997 Kentucky Derby Program

Autographed 2000 Kentucky Derby Program

Autographed Kentucky Derby 121 Signature Series Glass

Autographed 2002 Breeders' Cup Program

Twin Spires Club Survey---Earn up to 400 points!

Tell us what you think! Your feedback and comments help us make our product better than ever.

Take a moment to fill out the NEW 2003 Survey (Survey 2) on the Twin Spires club website, www.twinspiresclub.com. As a bonus your account will be credited with 300 points. You can earn an additional 100 points for completing the 2002 Survey (Survey 1).

Derby Store

Pick up official Derby merchandise to commemorate Funny Cide's victory in the Kentucky Derby!

Earn 10 points for every dollar you spend at the Derby Store!

Horse Hats

Use your Twin Spires Club points to purchase a horse hat of Derby winners and racing legends!

To be removed from this email list, please click here. Click here to view our Privacy Policy.

Reprinted with permission of Churchill Downs Incorporated.

Figure 9.2: Sample E-mail and E-newsletter

~~~~~~

WindStar Wildlife Garden Weekly e-Magazine

The Voice of Wildlife Habitat Naturalists

For the week of April 5, 2004

~~~~~~

THIS WEEK'S TOPICS:

~~~~~~

— Featured Article

— THE EVOLUTION OF A RAIN GARDEN

— EDITOR'S NOTES: Homecoming For Jenny Wren

— FROM WILDLIFE HABITAT FORUM: World Is My Backyard!

— GIVE THE GIFT OF NATURE

— ODDS 'N ENDS: A Thousand Points Of Green

— WANDERLOST: Migratory Routes Increasingly Threatened

— BIRD SONG RECORDINGS CAN ATTRACT BIRDS TO HABITAT

— QUOTATION OF THE WEEK: Edward Abbey

— EMERALD ASH BORER ERADICATION COST ESCALATES

— PLANTS THAT ARE FOR THE BIRDS

— BECOME A CERTIFIED WILDLIFE HABITAT NATURALIST!

— HABITAT TIP: How To Attract Bluebirds To Your Feeder

Dear Donna,

Welcome to WINDSTAR WILDLIFE GARDEN WEEKLY—

the FREE e-Magazine from WindStar Wildlife

Institute that will provide you with timely, interesting information on wildlife and how you can improve the wildlifehabitat on your property. And, we'll give you a look at what's new at the Institute and our web site: http://www.windstar.org

THE EVOLUTION OF A RAIN GARDEN

~~~~~~

By Wendi Winters

Corinne Reed-Miller is not your typical homeowner. She's deliberately removing her grassy lawn and has dug up her asphalt driveway to plant a vegetable garden. Ms. Reed-Miller, an Admiral Heights, MD resident, puts in a few more hours of work trying to save nearby Weems Creek, after a long week as a NASA computer engineer. (Photo by Corinne Reed-Miller shows part of the front yard that has been transformed with new plantings, pavers and mulch.)Her method is a little subversive: she's using her home as a showplace for rainwater conservation, native plantings and organic gardening.

"The main reason I am working toward 100 percent storm-water management on my own property is because poor storm-water management is the biggest environmental problem in urban watersheds," said Ms. Reed-Miller.

"Residences make up 47 percent of the Weems Creek Water-shed, so even if every single business did its part to

improve storm-water management, we'd still have an un-
healthy creek," she added. "We need the businesses to do
their part, but we have to do ours, too."

Ms. Reed-Miller's gardening methods, adapted from numerous
workshops sponsored by Bay Foundation, the Adkins Arbore-
tum and other like-minded groups, could be easily trans-
lated to homes of any size in this region.

In the process, instead of a tabletop of sunburnt grass,
she's creating a tableaux of year-round beautiful color
and varied texture that attracts birds, honey bees and
butterflies, yet takes very little effort to maintain.

"A typical 1,000-square-ft. roof sheds 600 gallons of
water in every one inch of rainfall," Ms. Reed-Miller
explained.

She originally placed 55-gallon drums at each corner of
her home, but was only catching and reusing 220 of the 600
gallons spilled from her roof in a storm. Ms. Reed-Miller
also found out that rainwater shedding from a summer
rooftop can be as hot as 140 degrees—not enough to boil a
crab, but enough to make him unhappy while encouraging the
growth of oxygen-grabbing algae.

Her solution has been to design and build rain gardens to
utilize the water pouring off her roof. She's built one

sized to catch all the rain from a 1-inch soaking and has plans for several more—one at each corner of her house and one or two more that will catch extra spillover from a storm.

In her rain garden she's planted a number of plants native to Maryland, including swampmilkweed because "it attracts Monarch caterpillars"; Joe-Pye weed, black-eyed Susans, Monarda fistulosa or wild bergamot since "Goldfinches like the dried seed in wintertime"; and inkberry bushes as "native pollinators like bees and butterflies are attracted to them." "I'm not a native freak," she laughed, pointing out her Lord Baltimore hibiscus, a hybrid, unlike the native marsh hibiscus.

Still, she draws the line at planting non-native invasive species like English ivy and mint. With some muscle provided by her son and some of his Annapolis High School buddies, she dug up the asphalt driveway. Where the top half once lay, she planted an organic vegetable garden. She placed gravel on the bottom half in an effort to reduce the impervious surfaces on her property.

Near her garden are a double compost heap and a pile of mulch. Kitchen vegetable scraps, such as peelings, egg shells and coffee grounds are dumped on the heap. They are then covered with a layer of mulch, to keep curious animals away. Within a few weeks, the compost is ready-made fertilizer.

Ms. Reed-Miller also is slowly removing her grassy lawn in a process called a "lasagna garden." To make her lasagna garden, she placed large pieces of corrugated cardboard on top of the grass and covered the cardboard with a one-inch layer of mulch. It is called lasagna because it is laid down in simple layers, like lasagna.

Then she waited.

Most of the front lawn disappeared, replaced with plant-ings, and flagstone walkways were placed atop the mulched areas. The following spring, the cardboard had degraded. Most of the grass had died off. The few stubborn sprouts that return, she weeds. "Weeding is way easier than mow-ing," she said.

She'd spend the winter months planning her shopping list and diagramming the location of each new plant on her home computer. Once spring was in full swing, Ms. Reed-Miller started digging.

She's planted a mix of shrubs, plants, perennials and bulbs. "I had to visualize three or four years ahead and space things for mature growth," she said. "Make sure you plant ground cover, too."

Some of her selections include red osier dogwood, ("It looks so red in the winter."), winter grasses ("For more winter interest."), witch hazel, split beard blue stem and Virginia wild rye. In her tree-shaded back yard, she's planning to put in wood oats, which thrive in a shady environment.

* * *

You may want to make your sender line seem more "human" by including phrases like "yourfriends@" or "the team@." Again, you're going to do whatever you can do to make this a conversation between one human being and another, rather than a monologue from an institution to an unknown audience.

Sample subject lines should also be clear and self-explanatory. Here are some samples:

- Half-Yearly Sale Begins Today!
- Free shipping on long-blooming perennials
- How old is your resume?
- Free eSeminar: "How To Reach Broad Audiences Through web-based Seminars" This is another example of a subject line that is too long and will get truncated on AOL.

Obscure or truncated sender addresses and subject lines are roadblocks to potential customers. Why open difficult or questionable material when other e-mails are clear and easy to access?

Another roadblock to good dialogue can appear after clicking to open an e-mail, when a window appears warning not to open the e-mail because it contains a picture. Additional links or warning screens are definite deterrents to e-mail success.

When Should You Send Your E-mail Marketing Message?
Studies show that the best days to send e-mails to *businesses* is Tuesday through Friday. Lunchtime is best time of day. Avoid sending mailings on busy mornings during catch-up time, when your message will seem a lot less important than your customer's own in-house memos, correspondence, orders, and so forth. Avoid sending messages on Fridays or weekends, when employees are eager to get out of the office. Many messages delivered on Friday won't be seen until the following Monday, when they are *most* likely to be overlooked, skipped, or even deleted in the midst of employees' usual start-of-week anxiety.

There are some exceptions to the Tuesday- through Friday lunchtime advice. For instance, if you are targeting business people with an offer of discounts related to live entertainment, dining, or leisure activities that take place on the weekend, then messages sent on Friday afternoons are fine. Be sure to consider the specific nature of your business or service.

E-mail messages should be sent to customer homes on weekends. The best time is late Sunday morning, when people are likely to be rested and have set aside time for leisure or home entertainment, which often includes surfing the net and checking e-mails.

What Is Your E-mail Marketing Message?
Here is Jupiter Communications' list of *What Consumers Want* in their e-mails*:

- Promotions and offers
- Site/product information
- Useful information
- Entertaining information

You know you need to offer consumers something they want, but suppose you can't give away your product. What can you dangle in front of potential customers?

According to *Accucast*, "Subscribers value e-mails that provide beneficial information." Consider offering related forms of entertainment, useful instruction, or solid information as a lure to customers. Newsletters or special reports are popular as consumer lures. You might offer one free month of your newsletter to new subscribers. You might have customers click-through to read valuable tips related to their business or business in general. Let's say you're marketing payroll applications software. You might offer tips for more efficient payroll operations, or simple steps to help reduce employee absences.

How Often Should You Send Your E-mail Marketing Message? Just as you would in a real live conversation, be personal, be entertaining, and be resourceful, but don't bombard your reader. How do you know how many e-mails to send? How often to follow up? Although there is no scientific answer, *Accucast* suggests that it's better to "err on the side of not enough e-mail, rather than send too many."

If you're worried about bombarding customers with too many mailings, you might consider "disguising" mailings, by putting some proposed mailings into different formats: send a series of daily or weekly consumer tips, or incorporate information into newsletters (Refer to the *Newsletters* chapter in this book.)

Remember that the customer is a valuable source of marketing research information, so don't be afraid to come right out and ask customers how often they prefer to receive messages. The most common preferences given by consumers for frequency of e-mails are:

- Frequent updates
- Monthly updates
- Contact when service updates are announced; new products are available

And don't forget to use your own common sense. Send e-mails only when the content deserves it; customers who see the same information repeating over and over will soon learn to avoid your e-mails, delete them, or unsubscribe and opt out completely.

Testing Your E-mail Campaign

Testing is a complex and variable endeavor. Volumes have been written on ways to categorize, tally, and sort test responses. Statistics are slippery devils and supposedly "hard" numbers can be manipulated to reflect different results.

Professional market researchers can provide simple or sophisticated testing services. The smart marketer is aware that testing can and should be tailored to each individual product, service, or company to ensure the most useful results.

You will definitely want to keep track of results of your e-mail marketing messages by following opt-out rates, for instance. At the very least, you should keep track of the frequency of mailings, and compare frequency to returns or purchases. You can design a survey, add response buttons to your web site, or build response capability into your e-mail message. Whatever the format, keep the survey process simple, easy, and user friendly.

The list of elements that can be tested on an ongoing basis is vast. The most basic elements to track might include:

Customer Identification Categorize customers who buy versus those who don't; number of click-throughs vs. hits, opt-ins vs. opt-outs, subscribers vs. non-subscribers.

You can further divide customers into endless demographic categories, such as age groups or gender.

Product Pricing Compare results of e-mails offering regular prices vs. discounts, special offers, or promotions. Track the results of sales vs. special limited time offers. Note differences in results when you change payment options, such as reducing or eliminating shipping charges, interest, or service fees.

Location Geography may play a part in the success of your mailings. You might categorize results by state or region, or compare city vs. suburb. If you have international dealings, you may need to consider the effectiveness of messages by country or language.

Scheduling Depending on the nature of your business, you may want to keep track of results by seasonal vs. year-round sales; responses before, during, or after holiday times; specific selling peaks, such as planting seasons, summer or winter vacation time, heating season, or cooling season, and so forth. For some products, testing sales by the day of the week or even the time of day may yield variable results.

Content Compare results by varying subject lines, return-sender lines, simple vs. detailed copy, chatty tone vs. formal tone, and so forth.

Format Consider testing HTML vs. plain text, single screen vs. multiple screens, graphics or no graphics and variations in layout or design. You might test the response differences between links at top, middle, or bottom, or even single links vs. multiple links. The number of variables is almost limitless. Intrepid journalist/marketing columnist Heidi Anderson offers a case study that shows how effective a simply designed e-mail marketing test can be.

Mini-Case Study: **Dessy**

Dessy, the company studied, is a well-known bridesmaid dress retailer. Their web site was successful and generated a satisfying level of online sales—on initial visits. Return visitor traffic lagged behind. Dessy turned to Portent Interactive for help.

As part of a web site redesign, Dessy began offering an opt-in news feature: customers had to sign up on the web site for special mailings, including promotional offers or unique information.

Customers who signed up became the subscriber base for the marketing test. Two small groups (ten to fifteen percent of the total database) were chosen randomly from the total database.

The first group of about 1,000 members received an e-mail with this subject line: "Live in Manhattan? Buy your bridesmaid dresses online!" Three hundred people opened the message, and of that group, 200 clicked-through to the site.

The second group of 1,000 people received the *same* message, with a different subject line: "Manhattan Residents: Buy your bridesmaid dresses online!"

The results? The first e-mail message, with the friendly, chatty subject line, generated a far greater response than the more abrupt second message. As a result, the first message was sent to the entire database and resulted in over 500 click-throughs.

Dessy tested another variable when it was time to market their "Look-Book," a glossy style publication displaying their latest designs and fabric swatches. The test mailing included a photograph of one dress.

The initial mailing cropped the photo to a small size to cut down on the download time. Of the 800 people who received the small photo e-mail, about 270 opened it, and only about fifty bothered to click-through to the site.

After those disappointing results, a second mailer, with a much larger photo, went out to another 800 people. Contrary to expectations, about 300 people, were intrigued enough to open the message. Of those 300 people, 100 clicked- through to the site, double the number for the first mailing.

Dessy sent the second mailing to its entire database of just under 10,000 people. It was opened by 2,800 people, and approximately 1,000 clicked-through.

Average sales had been between two to four units per day. After the mailing with the large photo, sales jumped to ten to twenty units per day. A great recommendation for testing.

The Web

As you know, this book is about integrating media in order to build and sustain a meaningful conversation with your customers. So, of course, there has to be a chapter about using the World Wide Web. After all, doing business online has become an absolutely critical part of the marketing mix, widely used and increasingly embraced by customers. But, consider this. If we had written this book just ten years ago, you wouldn't be reading a chapter about the web, because, as a marketing medium, it didn't really exist.

It's difficult to remember just how new the web as a marketing tool really is. But, its relative newness as a communications vehicle doesn't keep it from being one of the most effective tools for building, maintaining, and growing relevant conversations with your prospects and customers. In fact, the web has probably been the most influential medium in terms of building customers' expectations about how they want to interact with businesses. The web has caused a significant shift in the information paradigm. The user, your customer, controls when they get information and how much information they get.

This has carried over into the way customers perceive all media. In other words, if not for their newfound control online, they probably wouldn't be demanding as much control and relevance from your more traditional marketing communications.

There is a direct corollary between increased usage of the web and the current phenomena that marketers must face. People's attention spans are diminishing—using the web forces companies to get to the point, and customers expect us to get to the point more quickly in other media as well. There is assumed interactivity on the web that carries over to more traditional media, as well. Customers expect choice, selection, and an opportunity to specify preferences and offer feedback. Even the aesthetics of traditional media have been affected by the web. Cyber-influenced icons appear everywhere. Photo images often appear as they would onscreen.

In addition to the impact it's had on media in general, the web itself is big business. Just how big?

The Online Computer Library Center Office of Research estimates that there are currently close to ten million multi-page web sites. Some of these are personal sites—proud parents posting pictures of a new baby, fan sites dedicated to a favorite actor or rock star. But, most sites were built by businesses or organizations, and built specifically to facilitate transactions and foster ongoing dialogues.

According to the Direct Marketing Association, expenditures for interactive marketing are expected to reach $13.8 billion in 2005. In fact, annual growth rates for direct marketing expenditures from 2000–2005 will be highest for interactive marketing (11.6 percent per year), compared to radio (8 percent annually), television (6.9 percent), and telephone (6.6 percent).

Every day, an estimated 50 million people log on in the U.S. alone. And, that number is growing as well. So why do consumers use the web? To stay connected. To stay in the conversation.

Ultimately, the web is not an inexpensive alternative to print publishing or a new vehicle for paid advertising. Instead, the medium has evolved into something far more powerful. The web has become a marketer's dream, an automated way to connect to people one-to-one.

The Web Experience: The Ultimate Conversation

For some time there was a great debate in the online industry about whether "content" or "community" was more important. It appears today that "connectivity" eclipses both. If you follow the evolution of online giant America Online (AOL), you can see this process in action.

Over the years, AOL supported special interest groups and developed proprietary content. But today, the majority of AOL's twenty-five million members use the service as an Internet Service Provider (ISP). AOL enables them to send and receive e-mail and to access the Internet.

When the web first became popular a few years ago, consumers "surfed" for hours on end. Today, while spending less time online overall, the average consumer spends the largest portion of their online time swapping information—whether it's sharing tips about healthcare, sending a friend the latest music files and jokes, or keeping in touch through e-mails or chatting. The Internet has become a prime means of interconnection for large numbers of consumers who share their experiences. It's natural that this sense of interconnectivity extend to the companies with which consumers do business. In this chapter, we'll talk about how you and your web site can take advantage of the online conversation between your organization and consumers, *and* among consumers.

Critical to the success of any true conversation, communication on the web can and must be a "two-way street." Unlike most advertising media, the web can enable you to enjoy a real—and even real-time—dialogue with your visitors. Ask them for feedback and opinions. Have customers rate your current products or make suggestions for new offerings. Conduct online market research or collect demographic data. Whether you build-in something as simple as an e-mail feedback button or invest in a multimedia solution, engaging your visitors will enrich their online experience—and increase their loyalty to your brand.

What Makes the Web Unique in the New Marketing Conversation?

Compared to all other marketing media—from letters and catalogs to telemarketing, print, broadcast, and e-mail—the web is the only medium in which a significant portion of the audience *seeks out* the marketer. All other media operate by finding customers. A web site works best when it is found by customers.

Marketing over the web is not, as the abbreviation has it, B2C (business-to-consumer). It's C2B (consumer-to-business). People come to your web site with a goal in mind. It is the ultimate in active, cognitive engagement. The emotional appeals of broadcast and print advertising don't seem to work with web site visitors. Many of us immediately hit "Skip Intro" if we sense a creative, but unnecessary, animated opening coming. So, you can include attractive images, sound, or animations on your web site, but users arrive at your site looking for something; if it doesn't seem like they're going to find it, they leave. It's easy to sell them if you have what they are looking for. If you don't, it's difficult to even get their attention, much less sell them anything.

Here's another thing to keep in mind. "Surfing" isn't really a good metaphor for using the web. It's more of a "hunt," with something specific in mind. Consumers expect to find what they're looking for on the web. There's nothing more frustrating than visiting a web site and clicking and clicking, and coming up empty-handed. Figure out what your customers want. Ask, if you have to. Then, give them a quick, easy, and intuitive way to get there.

Companies that have figured out how to do this benefit from what are known as, "sticky web sites." Even if a user visits you for a quick answer to a simple question, you can encourage them to revisit or stay longer. How? By generating and featuring interesting information and attractive offers, plus compelling reasons to communicate back to you. Your site should leverage personalization and interactivity. Don't let a potential new customer wander away. The web is a user-driven medium—it's active, not passive. Your visitor won't stay in one place long. So when they keep moving, you want it to be within your site.

Remember, web users are coming to you. A potential customer is seeking you out; don't miss this opportunity. Ask yourself, what do they want? How can I keep them interested? What is compelling to them?

Redefining "Reach and Frequency"

The web offers unprecedented opportunities for companies to go to market without boundaries. Entrepreneurs and established companies alike are able to launch new ventures without the resources they would need to open traditional "brick and mortar" businesses. Online, small businesses can look bigger. You can market to customers anywhere in the world at any time. The web is truly a 24 × 7 medium; your site can be working for you, building relationships or closing sales, at night, holidays, and on weekends. These added business hours don't equate to added costs in terms of personnel or facilities. Your web site can also work for you across domestic and even international time zones. Again, this will save you significant costs whether you are selling products or providing online service to existing customers.

For some companies, there are also market segments that tend to be nocturnal buyers. Much like late-night infomercials, your web site can attract people who are awake when the rest of the world is asleep. This group can include insomniacs, of course, as well as college students, urban dwellers, high tech "geeks," and others.

From a consumer perspective, the web has provided unequalled access to goods and services. No matter what you're looking for, there is a good chance that someone somewhere is selling it online. Similarly, consumers can now comparison shop more easily and thoroughly than ever before, from the convenience of their home or office. In fact, many consumers who have not yet made regular online purchases use the web to compare their options before buying offline.

Understanding this particular application of the web can help you design features, functions, or sections of your web site that facilitate comparison shopping. Create charts that offer your features and benefits "at-a-glance." If appropriate, offer actual feature-to-feature comparisons between your product and the competition's. Post positive reviews or any third-party endorsements that speak to how and why your offering is better than the other options on the market.

Web sites have also made it easier and faster for consumers to collect and share information. Enhance this experience by providing multiple ways to download data, such as PDFs and text files. Encourage visitors to share the information they've uncovered with "E-mail to a Friend" functionality. Viral marketing among like-minded individuals creates instant "word-of-mouth."

Take Advantage of the Immediacy of the Web Right Now

Unlike other media, your web site can be posted, taken down, or changed almost instantaneously. This means that online, you can get feedback in real time; mark down (or increase) prices in real time; do business with virtual partners in real time; even streamline operations overall in real time.

The immediate nature of the medium has enabled marketers to address serious issues and/or opportunities far faster than they could have with more traditional media vehicles. Some examples of this can be categorized as "damage control." When celebrity homemaker and media mogul Martha Stewart was indicted for insider trading, she dedicated a web site, "MarthaTalks.com," to telling her side of the story. Less dramatic cases of this might include consumer information about a product or service recall, response to negative press, or even a sales event based on a current event. A retailer might promote a special offer on snowblowers to coincide with a major snowstorm. A change in the stock market triggers content changes on countless financial services sites.

A very productive use of the immediacy of web sites can be seen when fundraising groups use them to leverage the power of current events. Immediately after the terrorist attacks of September 11, 2001, millions of dollars in relief funds were raised online, and the Red Cross was able to use its web site to guide people to the nearest location where they could donate blood.

Integrating the Web with Other Media

Web sites can integrate with your other communications or operations, or they can stand-alone. Retail industry sites can be used in conjunction with brick and mortar stores by directing customers to the nearest location. They can function in addition to retail outlets—a customer may choose to research a product online and then visit a store for one last look before purchasing. Or, web sites can completely replace retail outlets by taking and tracking orders, with the added value of offering a full range of customer service including service by e-mail or through "live" (typed) conversations conducted through instant chats.

When you use more traditional media to converse with your prospects and customers, consider how your web site can complement that traditional touchpoint It's a good idea to include your URL in virtually all advertising and marketing. Consumers go to the web when they are curious or want additional information about products and services they have heard about. Anticipate the questions that a consumer might have after being exposed to a piece of marketing. Be sure to answer those questions—and continue the marketing conversation—when they arrive at your web site.

To generate response, URLs can be used in addition to, or in lieu of, toll-free numbers. A good example of this can be found in direct response radio advertising. Marketers who use this channel often face a conundrum. The best, and consequently most expensive, daypart in which to run radio is "drive time," when commuters become a captive audience in their car. However, it isn't always possible (or safe) for the prospective customer to respond via phone right there, and you can't count on them remembering a toll-free number. It is much easier to include an intuitive URL that relates to the offer and the creative they've just heard. For example, the call to action might be something as straightforward as, "Visit FreeHealthGuide.com for your free health guide." The same holds true for other response-driven media, such as television, outdoor, and transit.

When you do use the web as a reply mechanism, don't just direct the consumer to your company or product's general web site. Invest in unique microsites, landing pages, or "splash pages," specific to the offer you've made in the other medium. This will keep your conversation on course. It will also enable you to track response rates accurately.

Web sites can serve as fulfillment options when you are marketing a product or service that is a considered purchase. For example, ads for a new car can invite prospective customers to send a BRC or make a toll-free call and request a brochure. The same ad can offer the option of downloading the brochure via the web. This approach works particularly well when you are addressing an audience segment that is predisposed to conducting business online. Teens, for example, are often more comfortable with computers than their adult counterparts. But be certain that you understand and adhere to any privacy regulations regarding minors. We'll address privacy issues in general later in this chapter.

For many B2B marketers, the web has practically replaced printed collateral. This not only saves their companies money, but the option to download a PDF rather than wait for something to be mailed is considered a convenience by consumers.

You can also stay connected to these consumers after they've visited your web site via electronic newsletters, e-mail messages, or microsites which can themselves contain links to related sources of goods, services, and information.

Conduct Multiple Conversations with Multiple Audiences

At most companies, marketing communications professionals are charged with managing a variety of relationships—prospects, employees, investors, resellers, business partners, as well as different flavors of customers: new customers, loyal customers, lapsed customers. Fortunately, the web allows you to carry-on multiple conversations with multiple audiences concurrently.

That's why an important first consideration if you're building a web site is to plan for different tracks through it. Consider each "online persona," an individual profile of the type of person who is going to visit and benefit from your site. Why are they there? What are they looking for? How long are they willing to stay and look? Make sure they have a logical—and efficient—path through the information.

Remember, a prospective customer will become frustrated if they find content that is only relevant to current customers. Similarly, an existing customer will resent a site that assumes they have no relationship with you.

In mapping out your site, you need to accommodate the needs of these different visitors. A prospect may need basic information, a returning customer may want an update on shipping or information about add-ons to the product they've already purchased. Your site may also need to service franchisees or resellers. Depending on your business, you may want to build local affiliate sites or microsites that address the needs of suppliers or other business partners.

A few years ago, the trend was to make a business web site an all-you-can-eat buffet. Companies posted every document in their archives and judged their web site by the number of pages. While these massive sites were impressive, they were cumbersome. Visitors lost their way, ran out of patience and became frustrated with the experience—and with the company that provided that experience.

For today's most effective web sites, relative size is irrelevant. People visit and, just as importantly, revisit sites that make their lives easier, regardless of number of pages. The promise of the web is vast amounts of information, sorted through, and served up instantaneously.

For some companies and some audiences, a guided tour makes the most sense. We've seen companies post sites that are, in actuality, web-enabled slideshows. This can work well if your objective is extremely focused. For example, you might design a password-protected web site specifically for use by your sales force. When they have a prospect on the phone, they can walk them through a streamlined capabilities presentation.

Other companies create landing or splash pages that ask the visitor to identify him or herself. For example, a site selling travel insurance might ask whether you are a traveler or a travel agent. Once you click on the appropriate response, you are directed to content that fits your needs. Similarly, a site that educates people about college funding options might set up different paths for students, parents, and educators. For efficiency's sake, much of the content may be the same. But the path by which each category of visitor gets there differs.

One of the things people like about the web is that they get to control where they go and what they do. But, the importance of this sense of control shouldn't prevent you as a marketer from thinking through each visitor's logical progression and designing your site to match it.

Web mapping is a way of depicting the skeletal structure of your site.

A web map can be linear, looking very much like an outline, or more graphic in nature with shapes depicting different types of pages and content. It's helpful to overlay a mapping of a typical visit from each of your audience segments. This can help you ensure that customers, prospects and partners, or any other user can access the information they're looking for quickly and with a minimal number of "clicks."

Back to Basics: What's Your Online Objective?

Web sites can serve many masters. You can design a site that helps you build brand. You can generate leads by driving prospects to a site developed for that purpose. You can provide online fulfillment material. You can build a site that nurtures existing customer relationships. Web sites can be as targeted as any piece of traditional direct mail. Or, they can be as general as a corporate brochure.

First, articulate what your web site is offering and the best way in which to present it. As any good copywriter will advise, it's best to put these words in the second person or "you" voice. Imagine that you're speaking directly to the prospect or customer you would like to visit your site. What's in it for them? Information they can't find elsewhere? A fun and convenient way to shop? A chance to join a community of like-minded individuals? A timesaving way to conduct personal or professional business?

Once you determine what you are offering, make certain that your content and the structure of your web site align with it. If people come to you because they want to save time, design a site with intuitive navigation and use updated technology so they really do save time. People using the web are almost always in a hurry. If navigating your site—whether they are looking for information or products to purchase—appears to be difficult or time-consuming, you will lose them. Be sure you leverage technology to make return visits/purchases as streamlined as possible.

===

More About Having What Users Want: Offers

If you buy the premise that having what users want is the best thing you can do to build web traffic, then the question remains, what do users want? That's easy. They want relevant content, answers to questions, convenience, information—not advertising. And, they're only human; they want free stuff. Years of marketing experience have shown us that premium items work. Tee shirts, coffee mugs, alarm clocks, calculators, radios, baseballs caps, tote bags, and umbrellas have all been proven to engage people. If you create an offer that's attractive enough, the treasure hunters out there will find you.

But you can't run your web site like a direct mail campaign. Premiums that work well in direct mail won't necessarily work on a web site. Can a free coffee mug distract a web user who is looking for, say, an explanation of the difference between robusta and arabica coffees? That's hard to say. But if your site offers a page of information or a downloadable brochure about the difference between those coffees, you'll be in the crosshairs of that user's attention. We're back to that goal-driven, cognitive aspect of the web again.

The web is the ideal medium for customer education. Almost anything that makes your product or service special or unique could be the subject of a white paper. And the web is willing to distribute it for you at low cost, tirelessly, twenty-four hours a day, to people who want the information. But white papers just scratch the surface of stuff you can give away.

The offers you make via the web have to be interactive, too. How about a page that allows users to compare your product to that of several competitors, feature for feature? How about an archive of all past issues of your e-mail newsletter, fully searchable; an archive of articles about your organization that have appeared in different publications; a newswire for events in your market or industry; planning tools for purchase decisions; a guided tour; a discussion group; or a troubleshooting database? All these things are being offered to the public on web sites right now. Development costs for such items are not high, and the functions can be purchased ready-to-run in many cases. Distribution costs are very low, considering the exposure and reach the web provides.

If your product is information- or entertainment-based, like books, music, films, software, you can even provide prospects with downloadable samples or samples that can be played with a browser plug-in. This costs little more than the space to house the files, and you can even ask visitors to register before downloading, giving you a chance to request permission to stay in touch with them.

Remember, the overall marketing conversation must be perceived as *theirs*, not *yours*. The web offers countless ways to empower your customer.

"White mail," the name we give to those unsolicited requests for information about your products that come in through postal mail, has always been rare and precious. But on the web, white mail is the primary activity! Millions of people, all over the world, go to the web for information. An appreciable fraction of these people are asking for a sales pitch.

Some visitors come to your site in response to advertising that suggests you are selling goods and services they are looking for. But you will also have visits from people who have already bought from you and need follow-up service; people looking for free information (like reporters and analysts); people deciding whether to recommend you to their friends; people validating a decision they have already made to buy from you; people who have bought from you and love your product so much they want to know the latest news about it.

The list goes on and on. And, if these different types of visitors are important to your and your business, you'll have to make sure that your web site welcomes each and every one.

Effectively Conversing on the Web

In the English-speaking world, restrooms have universal identifiers: "Men" and "Women." But we've probably all had the experience of going to a theme restaurant that has renamed them to be clever. It may not be too difficult to figure out if you're a dog or a cat, a star or star-let, a sombrero or tiara, but why should you have to think about it? No-body enjoys clever restroom names enough to offset the irritation of having to think about which restroom door to use.

The principle is the same at your web site. When you make people think about how to get around, they won't appreciate your cleverness as much as they are irritated by the effort demanded of them.

Usability The first rule of web site development is to use standard terminology and conventions. You may think that underlined words look unattractive as links, but everybody knows what they mean. When you underline words that aren't links, you create user resentment. If you try to call your home page anything other than "home," you create user resentment. If you don't have a home page link on every page, you cre-ate user resentment. You get the message. If the user resents you, they're not very likely to join in a conversation with you.

Web users are attracted by pages that are easy to understand and navigate. The name of the game in web page design is usability. Visi-tors like web sites they find usable. They are well disposed to them, and they take pleasure in them, which helps the marketing conversa-tion succeed!

In 2002, web guru Jakob Nielsen updated his list of the most com-mon user irritants found on popular web sites.

Jakob Nielsen's Top Ten Web-Design Mistakes of 2002

1. No Prices
2. Inflexible Search Functions
3. Horizontal Scrolling
4. Fixed Font Size
5. Blocks of Text
6. Javascript in Links
7. Infrequently Asked Questions in FAQ
8. Collecting E-mail Addresses without a Privacy Policy
9. URLs over 75 Characters
10. "Mail to" Links in Unexpected Locations

Source: www.useit.com/alertbox/jakobnielsen.com

Looking at the list, there's a recognizable pattern. Many of these "mistakes" arise from wrongheaded attempts to control the user experience. One of the things people like about the web is that they get to control where they go and what they do. A second principle that can be discerned relates to trust. Providing a privacy policy when you collect e-mail addresses demonstrates openness and helps web visitors decide whether they can trust you. We'll discuss this in more detail later in this chapter.

Your priority, of course, is to make sure anyone using any kind of software can reach you, and maybe buy something from you. So, you have to make sure your web site and your server software use protocols that other kinds of software understand.

Fortunately, you and your technical people don't have to sort through volumes of protocols and specifications. There is a consortium that develops and promulgates standards for the web. The World Wide Web Consortium, also known as W3C, develops web standards to ensure access, interoperability, and future development.

Establishing Trust

Your web visitors may be looking for a great variety of information, products, services, solutions, and content. But, there is a common need. The need to trust.

Despite the continued growth of online users in the U.S. and worldwide, there are still a great number of people uncomfortable with conducting business online. They may be worried about privacy or fraud. They may just be more comfortable with a real person over a check-out counter or on the other end of a phone line. They may be skeptical about the viability of a business they know only via their monitor, keyboard, and mouse.

"Does the company really exist?" "Can they really deliver the goods?" "Can they really service and support my needs?" "Will they really be around the next time I visit them?" In developing and building your web site, you need to answer these questions with a resounding, "Yes, *really.*"

There are two ways to do this, and they are not mutually exclusive. Your visitor wants information, hard cold facts about the legitimacy of your business. At the same time, your visitor wants reassurance that they are making the right decision to proceed, and that they will be taken care of. You must satisfy both the rational and the emotional sides of your prospective customer.

In terms of establishing rational credibility, you can use many of the same techniques you would use in more traditional media. Talk about how long you've been in business and the history of the company. Use testimonials, reviews, or third-party endorsements when you can. Include a photo of your offices, a retail location, or individual products if appropriate. And, highlight—in a believable way—your absolute commitment to customer satisfaction with a liberal "no questions asked" guarantee.

Next, you need to appeal to their emotional side by giving your web site the personal touch; make it a human experience. You should show real people: the founders, the officers, customer service representatives, or customers themselves. And, again, be sure to showcase your unconditional, money-back guarantee. No, that's not a typo. The wonderful thing about a guarantee is that it appeals to both the head and the heart.

Earlier in this chapter, we noted that the web is the only marketing medium in which the customers seek out the vendor. Make it easy for them to communicate with you! Here's a "best practice" for you to consider. To make your visitors feel especially welcome and appreciated, include a "Contact Us" e-mail link and make sure any messages to that address get answered within an hour. And take the messages seriously. Every message from a prospective or existing customer is an attempt to establish contact with your company, a precious event.

Many web sites automate response to e-mails for efficiency's sake. Meanwhile, most customers would rather communicate with a real person, especially about things like service issues. Think about how you can incorporate your employees into the customer's web experience rather than obviously impersonal contacts or e-mail addresses, such as "info@xyzcompany.com." There will be times when this is not practical, but it's worth the effort to consider it. After all, this is a marketing conversation and nothing beats the power of a real person. Online or off.

Respect and Your Customers' Privacy "Respect." Aretha Franklin wasn't singing about marketing on the web, but, she certainly tapped into a basic human want. Your customers want you to respect their personal information and privacy. They want you to appreciate their business and provide them with secure online transactions.

According to Forrester Research, "Ninety-two percent of companies feel that they adequately protect users' privacy by disclosing practices and not selling data. However, ninety percent of sites fail to comply with . . . basic privacy protection principles."

There are several resources that can help you adhere to the best practices of online privacy policies. The Online Privacy Alliance (OPA) is a cross-industry coalition of more than eighty global companies and associations committed to promoting the privacy of individuals online. The Alliance works to define privacy guidelines and to promote a more secure online environment for users. Its members include such companies as AOL Time Warner, IBM, and Microsoft, as well as organizations like American Advertising Federation, American Association of Advertising Agencies, and even the United States Chamber of Commerce.

At the OPA web site, www.privacyalliance.org, you can download a helpful pamphlet entitled, "Creating Consumer Confidence Online: Five Essential Elements to Online Privacy." The elements the title refers to include:

- Adoption and Implementation of a Privacy Policy
- Notice and Disclosure
- Choice and Consent
- Data Security
- Data Quality and Access

In general, a typical Privacy Policy might read something like this:

We value our customers and your privacy is important to us. (YOUR COMPANY) will never sell, rent, trade, or give your e-mail address or any other personal information to any outside party for any purposes whatsoever.

Should you have any questions about this policy, please contact NAME@URL.com.

It's important to give the visitor a way to respond to your policy. This not only fosters a two-way conversation, it also proves that you will stand behind the policy. The fact that a real person is available to discuss the policy creates a sense of trust.

The Ins and Outs of Opting-In and Out There are some situations in which you, as a marketer, might want to share your web visitors' information. For example, if you manage a web site that offers parenting information to new mothers, you might have promotional partnerships with manufacturers of diapers or baby formula. These companies are eager to reach the same audience.

In a situation like this, the second and third points listed above become important: "Notice and Disclosure," and "Choice and Consent." If your program includes sharing, renting, or selling visitor information, give your visitor the option to participate or not. Explain the situation in clear language, with a marketer's focus on the benefits to your visitor. For example, your site can include language like,

NewMomNews.com sometimes shares visitor information with promotional partners offering products and services for new mothers. If you are interested in receiving special offers from these companies via e-mail, please indicate "Yes" below. If you do not want to participate, please indicate "No," and we will not share your information.

Basically, whenever you plan to include a visitor in any outbound communications program, you need their permission. This is called their "opt-in." Conversely, you need to give them a way to decline or "opt-out" of inclusion in the program. And the process of offering a chance to opt-in and/or opt-out must be continual. Not only is it proper online manners, but it retains the trust and respect that are intrinsic to an ongoing marketing conversation.

Remember, for consumers, much of the web experience is about choice. That's why the concept of "opting-in" and its counterpart "opting-out" is such an important one. This process has become the online world's most tangible demonstration of respect for users.

Make Certain Your Web Site is Safe and Secure

Another component in establishing trust is ensuring that personal information collected and transactions conducted on your web site are secure. How do you do this? In two steps, ensure that their data and online activity are secure, and then promote the steps you've gone through on their behalf. This is a great way to prove that you have their best interests in mind and are committed to earning their trust.

It is also your responsibility to ensure that any third party partners adhere to the same security standards. If, for example, you have outsourced the "check out" function of your ecommerce site, you'll want to research the vendor's security practices and review their track record with other clients.

VeriSign is a company that has done a good job communicating the importance of online security to consumers and marketers alike. Addressing both sets of needs has helped VeriSign become the top player in its market. In fact, VeriSign manages billions of secure transactions each day. Most of the Fortune 500 companies use some of VeriSign's services. Smaller companies can choose to build a secure web site through VeriSign's Network Solutions subsidiary.

From a technology standpoint, there are many security solutions on the market today. The ISP hosting your site should be able to help your technical staff find the one that's right for your particular application.

Communicating on the Web

Chances are you're a web user yourself. So, when you're writing for the web, bear in mind how you read from the web. You glance at the page, scan the headlines, look for something specific (it's why you went there), read some of the copy, and make a choice. You're not alone; this is the pattern that most users follow. Your own web site can facilitate this process by anticipating the choices your visitors are looking for, making it easy to find them and continue moving.

Quite simply, computer screens are not printed pages. According to Jakob Nielsen, eyes move 25% slower across monitors than across a printed page. And, not surprisingly, most people (estimates start at 79%) scan a web page rather than reading it. A shorter page will also load more quickly—an important element in your average visitor's overall satisfaction.

That's why, when writing for the web, you need to get to the point quickly. This isn't the time for storytelling or painting a picture with words. With that said, the rules for good copywriting still apply. You are still speaking directly to a person. It's still one-to-one communication.

When you write or evaluate web copy, there are nine general principles to keep in mind according to copywriter/consultant Jeff Laurie of Cambridge, Massachusetts:

Principle 1. The Web is Personal, Private, and Intimate
Address the web visitor as "you" and keep the copy conversational. Treat the intimacy as a trust. Your technology may be able to identify information about visitors that seems highly personal, such as which browser they are using. If you refer to such information, you will make a lot of your visitors nervous. When a customer is asking, "How did they know that?" he or she is thinking less about the marketing conversation and more about other issues.

Principle 2. The Web is Voluntary Multimedia
The web was originally intended as a medium for text, but it has evolved beyond that. And sometimes text isn't sufficient to communicate. Use images generously. Take advantage of video and sound, but *always* give the user the choice of whether to open the audio or video file. Remember how many people may be in crowded offices when they access your site. The last thing they may want is a chorus of "Louie Louie" or even the Toccata and Fugue.

Principle 3. The Web Is Inherently Interactive Going online is something people *do.* Your visitor expects to act, to click, to jump from screen to screen. Don't try to provide all the information on one screen. Give them opportunities to jump around, but design the site so a person is never more than three clicks from what he might want.

Principle 4. The User Is in Control As we've said several times, your visitors have sought you out. You are a stop on their journey. They are willing to put in the effort to get what they want from you (although you have to make it as easy as possible), but if you try to control their activities, you'll probably lose most of them.

Principle 5. The User Is Conditioned to Look for Options The web user's expectations are high, but attention span may be low for anything other than what he or she is looking for. When you write for web users, be aware that even while they're reading your copy, they are looking around the page for some indication of what they should do next.

Principle 6. Hyperlinks Are Built-In Action Devices Unlike direct mail, where copywriters expend enormous energy trying to find ways to get prospects involved, on the web, they already *are* involved. Clicking a hyperlink is a conscious decision, much more so than any other kind of marketing interaction.

Principle 7. It Costs Money to be Online Especially for users on dialup connections (still the dominant access technology), your prospects are paying to read your promotion. They are unforgiving of copywriters who waste their time. Organize concepts clearly, write tersely.

Principle 8. There Are No Built-In Affinity Groups The channel that brings the user to you is the same channel that can take the user to millions of other web sites. You may think you have developed a "community" at your site, and you may have to a certain extent, but the cognitive nature of the web tends to reinforce individuality.

Principle 9. Web Pages Are Units of Thought If you want to tell your story, you must organize it into scenes and chapters. Each web page should be focused on a critical term, no more than two or three words long. If that critical term is a keyword you came up with when you did your search engine analysis, then your site will organize itself around principles of "findability" as well as conceptually manageable chunks. Copywriting should be pared down from writing you do for print media. Think of scanning—heads, subheads, bulleted lists, links to more information, easy escape routes, details.

More Ways to Make the Most of Your Online Conversation

The web offers marketers endless opportunities for cross-selling. Thousands of individual sites target consumer groups engaged in identifiable activities. Marketers can take advantage of today's instant online communication options to locate these consumers in the process of shopping for related items and services. People visiting home-buying sites, for instance, are regularly wooed by pop-up offers for mortgages, home improvement products, even new cars.

Some creative marketers have added an element we call, "edutainment" to their online presence. If there is a way to deliver your message that entertains as it educates, you are going to have a very satisfied visitor. Smart, tasteful, relevant, well-executed humor, as in any and all media, can help you build a strong relationship with customers.

Other companies are taking advantage of new media categories that have emerged online, such as *advergames*. Since 2001 sales of video-game hardware and software ($9.4 billion) exceeded Hollywood box-office receipts ($8.35 billion), major advertisers like Burger King, Ford, and IBM have enthusiastically jumped onto the advergame bandwagon.

Keith Ferrazzi, president and CEO of YaYa LLC, the Los Angeles-based firm that produced advergames for the above clients, says "Games are not just about entertainment anymore . . . We have a new medium that is fundamentally different and . . . allows a company to enter into a relationship with a new consumer right there in the medium."

YaYa's data shows that an impressive 90 percent of consumers who received e-mail challenges visited the site and played that particular game. What's more, players routinely forwarded the games to a friend. Says Ferrazzi, "That level of peer-to-peer marketing is unparalleled."

If You Build It, Will They Come?

So much effort is invested in building a web site that it's tempting to assume the line from the film *Field of Dreams* applies here as it did to Kevin Costner's cornfield ballpark. "If you build it, they will come." Truth is, build it and they won't come if they can't find it. With so many millions of choices and potential paths online, you'll need to actively drive people to your web site.

Second, getting visitors means making the site easy to find. There are three basic ways to do this: 1.) through search engines, 2.), through integrated traditional and electronic marketing media, and 3.) by creating a "buzz" and allowing word of mouth to increase visits.

Getting on the Good Side of Search Engines Most people will use some type of search engine to look for you. It is true that you can advertise on the pages of search engines, and you can even gear your ad to certain keywords, so that people searching for that word will see a page with your ad on it.

But at this point most web users can recognize ads, and they accord more credibility to the actual search results than to the ads surrounding them. So, although advertising on top flight search engines may be part of your "getting found" strategy, you should put the lion's share of your efforts into creating a site that will appear among the top hits in a search.

Backing this up, a 2001 study by NPD Group (reported on the web site, NUA Internet Surveys: www.nua.ie/surveys/index.cgi) showed that search listings worked better than advertising for brand recall, favorable opinion rating, and inspiring purchases. "In unaided recall, search listings outperformed banners and buttons by three to one, and more than twice as many people gave a more favorable opinion of companies in the top three search positions than those featured in ads."

The study also showed that more than half (55%) of online purchases originated in search listings, as opposed to less than a tenth (9%) originating in ads.

Online search is now a big business—in two different ways. First there is an entire sub-industry of search engine optimizers (SEOs), organizations that consult with web developers on improving the odds of getting found by the search engines. Second, there is a lively trade in paid search placement. There is even one vendor (Overture) that does business on a pay-for-performance model—you only pay for users who actually click on the link to your site. In paid search placement, you pay a fee to be among, say, the first five hits for some keyword.

But there is no payment for search results on the world's premier search engine, Google, which may be one of the reasons that it is the world's premier search engine.

And, if you have any doubt about how important search engines are, consider this. If your site appears high in the rankings of Google and Yahoo!, you cover more than 75% of searches, worldwide.

Assuming you've done your best to make sure your web site has what the users want, the way to rank high in the search results is to have text on your pages that matches the text in the queries people enter in the searches. That means anticipating how users will phrase their queries. Then, use these exact words and phrases in heads, subheads, titles, and text.

The search engines also rank you based on your online affiliations, your overall presence on the web. For example, Google's primary ranking method for where a site appears on a search list is the number of links to that site from other sites.

Getting the Word Out—Marketing your Web Site

Sometimes, at least at the beginning, it's helpful to think of your web site itself as a product to promote. You can direct customers to your site through a mix of electronic media, such as e-mails, banner ads, and affiliated links. Also consider using direct mail, print and broadcast ads, statements, product inserts, and your company's collateral materials.

Again, to truly integrate your media and, thereby, your conversation, include your URL—and a compelling reason why they should visit—on any and all marketing you do. Driving people to your web site for "more information" is expected and appreciated.

Creating a Buzz Word-of-mouth is the advertising that money can't buy, and, it's especially important when it comes to web sites. Here's where connectivity can work to your advantage. With a relevant offer or offering, your satisfied visitor will naturally e-mail your URL to his or her friends. Anyone who has ever received a viral e-mail can tell you that the overall effect can be exponential.

Another good reason to encourage visitors to spread the word for you is that it adds to your credibility. Which would you trust: An e-mail from an online retailer talking about itself or an e-mail from a friend who just had a positive experience there?

Sometimes all it takes to create an advocate is to plant the idea. As you review your site or your e-mail marketing, consider where you can add an "E-mail to a Friend" button.

So, Who's Doing It Right, Right Now?

From a marketing perspective, some of the most exciting things happening on the web are the result of understanding visitors and then leveraging the unique capabilities of the online medium to provide an enhanced experience. Here are just a few examples.

It's unlikely that your business is of the size and scope of Amazon.com. But the web's most popular shopping destination does so many things right, there are lessons to be learned regardless of your own web project. Launched as an online bookstore in 1995, today's Amazon.com sells everything from computer equipment to apparel to more books than any other outlet anywhere in the world. The site is convenient and easy to use, and nicely intuitive in its search capabilities. It gives customers multiple ways to interact, from registering for gifts with an online "Wish List" to writing and posting reviews, from an e-mail suggestion box to making purchases and tracking delivery. All of these are supported by the site's expansive database. When a customer visits Amazon.com, they know they can get in, get what they want, and get back out in short order. It's another form of trust—trusting that the experience will be consistent—that's critical to a commercial web site's continued success.

When users visit Amazon.com, they may be looking for books. But when they visit AmericanSingles.com, they're looking for love. AmericanSingles.com has fast become one of the Internet's most active dating sites, with millions of registered single men and women. It's a friendly, easy-to-use site which establishes trust right away with the assurance that they've "been on the scene since Internet dating began." The marketers behind AmericanSingles.com seem to understand what their audience wants, with many interactive features like creating and posting a profile, searching for potential "dates," e-mail, instant messaging, and live chat. And, round-the-clock "customer care consultants" make the experience a bit less threatening to the novice.

Once you've found your dream date, you may want to book a romantic vacation for two. Between airline, hotel, and resort sites, there are plenty of ways to do this online. Most consumers turn to the travel portals, like Expedia.com and Travelocity.com. Ranked highest by consumers, Expedia.com has the advantage of being online longest, but both sites receive high ratings for customer satisfaction. Major parts of the appeal are their no-nonsense design, a robust database of individual travel preferences and transaction histories, searchable itineraries, and live travel agent back-up. A relative newcomer is Orbitz.com, which positions itself as the source for off-price travel packages. All of these sites save the consumer time and effort by removing the "middle man," or, in this case, the travel agent.

Another reason people go online is because they believe that if they "do it themselves" and put a bit of effort into the hunt, they can find better deals. Sites like eBay.com and PriceLine.com have been built on this particular attraction of the web. In both cases, the companies have created a perceived community of savvy bargain-hunters through mass media advertising. These sites offer feedback mechanisms, but both recognize that the main reason the visitor is there is to transact. There is very little descriptive copy. There are very few graphics. Visitors are there to strike a deal, and those deals are front and center on the site. While neither of these sites is likely to win a creative competition, they have won their customers' loyalty with their straightforward and businesslike approach.

Maybe you don't have multiple millions to build an online powerhouse like the ones we've described. But, you can still use the web in innovative ways designed to achieve your unique marketing objectives. In the B2B space, for example, your web site can serve as a bridge between a company's different operational functions.

Jim Delande, a Marketing Director at GTE Internetworking, found an innovative way to bring Sales and Marketing together online. Like many companies, GTEI was challenged by a relationship between its Sales and Marketing teams that was less than optimal. Marketing thought that Sales wasn't following up on good leads and Sales thought that Marketing wasn't generating good leads.

Delande pulled together a focus group of some of the company's top sales reps and asked what specific information they would most like to know about a lead before they followed up. Answers included implementation timing, budget, legacy systems, and technical compatibility.

With the aid of agency Direct Results Group, Delande developed a microsite with navigation built around the sales reps' hot buttons. A direct mail package was sent to prospects, driving them to the microsite with a downloadable white paper offer. Once there, the site collected data and also tracked where they went and how long they stayed. When this lead was handed over to Sales, there was a record of exactly what the prospect was interested in. The rep who followed up could use the knowledge to engage the prospect in a more targeted and relevant conversation.

An example of an organization that has leveraged the peer-to-peer possibilities of the web is WARM2Kids.com. Founded by Boston Celtics legend M.L. Carr, WARM2Kids, which stands for "We're All Role Models 2 Kids," is an online community providing tools to inform, instruct and inspire teens and young adults to make positive life decisions.

Besides reaching out to young people where they live—in front of their PC—WARM2Kids has taken advantage of online connectivity to link users to celebrity role models from the worlds of professional sports, music, television, government, and other high profile careers. Kids get to connect with these people as they explore topics ranging

Figure 10.1: GTE Internetworking

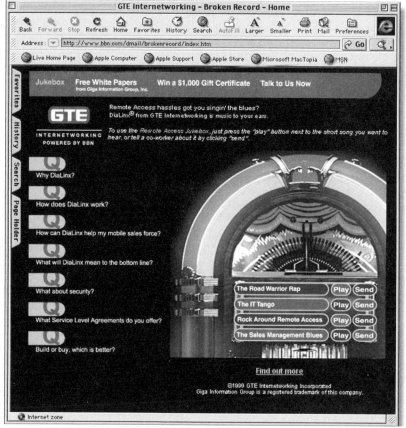

Reprinted with permission of GTE Internetworking.

from first dates to suicide. Because the experience is web-based, members can connect anonymously and in private, an important ingredient for helping young people.

For M.L. Carr, the WARM2Kids web site is clearly a labor of love. He states that, "If my legacy is that I won a couple of NBA championships with the Boston Celtics, and I played with people like Larry Bird and Dennis Johnson, then I haven't done my job." The organization has also attracted partners and sponsors from the business world, such as New Balance, the Sharper Image, COMP USA, and Hertz.

All of these sites—and countless others—are engaging consumers in an old conversation in some exciting new ways.

Figure 10.2 Warm2Kids

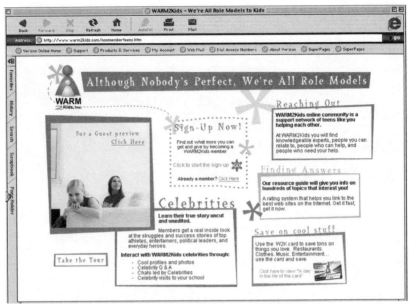

Reprinted with permission of Warm2Kids.

Some Succeed and Some . . . Well . . . Don't

What marketers have missed the boat? Overcomplicated the experience? Alienated their prospects and customers? Chances are, anyone who uses the web will have a horror story to share: Sites that are unforgiving and don't allow the visitor to correct a misstep. Sites that are over-art directed and too confusing. Sites that ask for too much personal data too soon in the conversation. E-commerce sites that crash at check-out—irretrievably emptying a shopping cart after the user has invested way too much time shopping. We won't name names here. What we will do is discuss a handful of the potential—and all too common—pitfalls and how you can prevent them.

If Your Site is Out-of-Date, You will be Out-of-Mind

Fast Your web site has to be current. Online, people expect "news" to be both new and newsworthy. You lose your credibility fast when a visitor finds outdated material on your site. If you can't commit to frequent—continual really—updates, don't build sections like "This Week's Special," "Calendar of Events," or "What's New?"

This brings up an important operational issue. The web site needs to be someone's—as in, one individual's—responsibility. There can be many contributors, and you can even use software that allows non-technical people within your own organization to update content. But, a specific person should be charged with keeping the site fresh, relevant, and usable.

They Found You, So Why Make Their Life Difficult?

The best web sites make life easier, not harder. For most consumers, the web is perceived as a time-saver. Think about the possible applications and alternatives. To conduct research, a person can head to a library, work with a librarian or a catalog system, find the facts they're looking for, and head back to their desk. Or they can turn to the web. Shoppers can drive downtown or to their local mall, hunt down the appropriate retailer, find the item they want, stand in line, pay, and drive home. Or they can turn to the web.

The structure and content of your site must convey convenience and ease of use right from the start of the online experience. From your home page through each and every path a visitor takes, you need to anticipate their needs and provide them with an efficient, streamlined way to meet them.

Please Don't Forget: The Web is Interactive

Visitors get frustrated, quickly, with sites that talk at them with no opportunity for interaction. Even the sleekest, most well-written web site is a missed opportunity if it doesn't begin or move the marketing conversation forward.

We spoke earlier about the importance of connectivity when people sit down at their computers. By visiting your site, a prospective customer is taking a first step toward connecting with you, your company, and your offer. Make the most of this with contact information, e-mail feedback mechanisms, surveys, chats, and other content that demonstrate that you want—and value—their opinion.

Never "Blind Them with Science" Showing off technologically is almost never a good idea online. Sure, it's fun to design with great graphics and Flash animation, but if your site takes too long to download or crashes the user's system altogether, you've just lost a conversation, and quite possibly a customer.

Unless you are a high tech company, speaking to a high tech audience, save the "bells and whistles" for another venue. As with any medium, put yourself in your customers' shoes. Think about their skills and the systems they are working with and build your site to accommodate their comfort level and any technical limitations.

This advice can help in a more holistic way as well. If you have done a good job defining your ideal customer or prospect, go ahead and immerse yourself in their online experience. Consider why they go to the web in the first place. Visit the sites they visit most often. This will help you understand what they expect in terms of content, complexity, and functionality.

When All Else Fails, Remember It's a Conversation

The best marketers have always understood the same basic principles of selling: listen, empathize, and offer relevant solutions to problems. Beyond any traditional medium, the web offers a more dynamic, real-time, and interactive way to converse with customers. Understanding how to take advantage of this no longer new media has made all marketers think like direct marketers.

The web is just about as one-to-one as you can get with a customer without picking up the phone or showing up on their doorstep. So, establish their trust, get personal, be interactive, and, by all means, give them what they're looking for.

Your web site can be the means of fostering an enduring dialogue with prospects, customers, and any other audience. That's why harnessing the power of the web is a critical key to the success of your new marketing conversation.

Wireless

According to an often-repeated story, a reporter sent an economically phrased question by wire to Cary Grant's agent. The telegram said, "HOW OLD CARY GRANT QUERY." Cary Grant himself decided to send the answer: "OLD CARY GRANT FINE STOP HOW YOU QUERY."

Every conversation provides room for humor and, more important for the marketer, misunderstanding. Just as conversations held in a recently acquired foreign language can be halting, the conventions of a new communication medium can present surprising and unwanted challenges

The more technologically proficient our society becomes, the more "tied in" to each other through such devices as cell phones, PDAs, laptops, and the Internet, the more our own and our prospects' needs for privacy and silence grow.

While wireless options continue to expand, wireless is not yet as universal as mail or the telephone. Even cell phones have not yet achieved complete market saturation. The U.S. lags behind Europe and Japan in wireless subculture. For the sake of discussion, we will focus on cell phones and the wireless web in this chapter.

The Wireless Marketing Scenario

A few years ago, there were some predictions and scenarios advanced for wireless technology. Since a wireless network can pinpoint the geographic location of a wireless device, a number of conjectures were made about advertising based on proximity. Conference speakers and other visionaries imagined a world in which a store might send a wireless message to any device passing by on the street.

Spam and outbound telemarketing may be viewed as intrusive in the world of e-mail and telephone. There is potential for even more intrusion in the wireless world. It doesn't matter how good your offer is. Users consider their wireless devices to be highly personal items, almost like an article of clothing. They often carry them everywhere, and most people don't like the idea that they are being tracked in their movements by advertisers.

Send unsolicited advertising to a cell phone—either voice or message—and you're asking for serious trouble. Spamming cell phones and PDAs is the kind of practice that will send consumers everywhere to the barricades. In fact, a 2002 white paper from Carat Interactive stated, "Outbound telemarketing to one's cellular phone is virtually a crime."[1] And wireless users don't perceive a great deal of difference between unsolicited voice calls and unsolicited text messages. From their perspective, their personal device is being invaded either way.

Like so many other aspects of the marketing conversation, wireless marketing is about maintaining and cultivating customer relationships. That means the conversation's simply not effective if it's not wanted. Your customers only want to hear from you when they expect to hear from you or when it is convenient to them. That means it can be acceptable if your message arrives in the right context or because the customer has asked for it. But broadcasting messages to compiled lists of wireless users offering weight loss preparations, inkjet cartridges, online gambling, sexual performance enhancement, or "hot pics," are even less likely to work in the wireless world than they do in e-mail. Given privacy considerations, outbound telemarketing to cell phones doesn't seem the best way to initiate an effective dialogue.

Texting in the Marketing Conversation

You text someone via the short messaging system (SMS). As we write this, about one-third of U.S. cell phones are SMS-enabled. An SMS message can be no longer than 160 characters, which becomes a major limitation of texting as a marketing medium. In fact, this limitation recently inspired political action. As the country was headed into the

2002 mid-term elections, an ad agency that specializes in political ads requested permission from the Federal Election Commission to omit the standard campaign disclosure, the "paid for by" notice, from SMS political ads, so more of the limited character space could be used for the candidate's messages. The Federal Election Commission granted the request.

Because SMS messages are so short and cell phone users compose them with a thumb on a tiny keypad, the SMS subculture developed a whole language of abbreviations. It's tedious to try to tap out on a cell phone keypad, "It was an excellent party last night. 'Can't talk. My parents are watching. I'll see you later." But you can get the same thing across with "XLNT PRT LST NITE. PRW. CUL8R."

Texters use many such abbreviations, as well as the full complement of emoticons popularized in online forums and e-mail, such as :-) for "I am smiling." But the abbreviations and the emoticons may not last because many cell phones now feature predictive text, which greatly facilitates sending complete words and phrases. When the Federal Election Commission was hearing the request for the exemption from campaign disclosure, it briefly considered requiring an abbreviation, such as "PD 4 BY JOHN JONES 4 CNGRS" but rejected the idea because it was afraid it would be swept into the position of setting standards for and evaluating abbreviations. The only reasons you might use abbreviations in a wireless marketing message are if the message doesn't fit the 160-character limit or you want to look really hip to a specific, generally young, audience. But be advised: "hip," like the word itself, can suddenly look awfully square.

Marketing Messages in the Wireless Arena

Assuming that you have invitations to send your messages to your wireless customers, how do you write them? With a 160-character limit, our five-step method for formulating your marketing message isn't going to work particularly well.

In fact, with your budget of 160 characters, you must find ways to combine all five steps into a single one. Additionally, your 160-character budget includes the "From:" and "Subject:" lines as well. Some services simply deduct fifty characters for them. Thus, the AT&T Wireless Messaging Center on the web limits your message body to 110 characters. You must also keep in mind that cell phone displays vary. Some screens can only display four lines with fifteen characters per line at a time.

This kind of message is what the Wireless Advertising Association would describe in its guidelines as a "full message" ad, i.e., one that uses the full 160 characters of an SMS message. The Association also describes a "sponsorship" message, which would contain up to thirty-four characters (no more than three lines of text on most phones). A sponsorship message would ride with some content the user presumably wants: sports scores, news headlines, or stock quotes.

The following example explores the limitations of SMS, using the AT&T Wireless Messaging Center on the web for messaging from an auto service center. Auto service centers often send various kinds of offers to their customers based on projections of the customers' mileage. When the software predicts that John Q. Public is due for a 3,000-mile oil change, it sends a letter or flyer, often with an accompanying coupon, to John Q. Public to try to get him to bring his car in. This seems to be a fairly effective strategy by regular mail, judging by the number of car dealerships that do it.

Theoretically, with SMS and cell-phone-equipped customers who have *invited* (very important) such a reminder service, it should be much easier and more immediate. Instead of putting an expiration date on the coupon, you should be able to tell the customer: "$10 off today only!"

The Offer The offer includes a front-end premium of a free cup of coffee. The fulfillment premium is a $10 savings on an oil change, provided either as a discount or a rebate.

The Customer Benefit The principal benefit of oil changes is in protecting the value of your car. There are other benefits: the car will last longer and it may run more economically. But these latter benefits are subsumed under the benefit of trade-in value, which looks like money in your pocket. And with SMS, we aren't going to have the chance to show more than one benefit.

If this were e-mail or traditional direct mail marketing, we would compose a wordy message including a headline, probably something like this:

To: John Q. Public

From: Baier Stein Direct

Regular Oil Changes Protect the Trade-in Value of Your Car And You Can Start Cashing It In Now!

Your owner's manual advises you to change your car's oil every five thousand miles. But several important studies have shown that regular three thousand-mile oil changes can actually increase your car's value at trade-in time. A car with a history of three thousand-mile oil changes runs better and more economically and is less likely to need maintenance. Buyers know that, and they will pay more for cars that have been protected with frequent oil changes. That's why dealers allow more for them in trade.

If you come in this week for an oil change, we'll let you start cashing in that extra value now! We'll give you back $10 for changing your oil! Come in now. It's worth money to you.

Sincerely,
Floyd Kemske
Service Manager

P.S. Call xxx-xxx-xxxx today and make an appointment for your oil change. This $10 rebate offer is only good until March 1. Have a free cup of coffee on us when you come for your oil change. We've just installed a gourmet coffee machine for our customers. Your first cup during a service visit is free!

This message is 928 characters. The only way to send it by SMS is to break it up into six messages, which is obviously unacceptable.

Here's our best attempt to get the same message into 160 characters:

To: John Q. Public

From: Baier Stein Direct

Subject: $10 Off Oil Change

Free coffee! Oil change protects your car's trade-in value. Save
$10 2day only.

What happens when this message reaches the customer on a typical
cell phone? Bear in mind that a cell phone screen can only display four
lines at a time with a maximum of fifteen characters per line.

First of all, the user must select the message from a menu, and the
only identification it has in that menu is the name of the sender. The
menu allows only one line for the sender's name, and it suppresses the
rest with an ellipsis (. . .). So when this message arrives, it appears in
the menu like this:

Baier_Stein_

Tip number one for texting: *Figure out how to say who you are in fifteen characters.* When the user chooses the message, the entire name of
the send appears, but unless it is an e-mail address, the system will add
an "at" sign (@) and an IP address (four quartets of numbers separated
by periods). Tip number two for texting: *use an e-mail address to identify the sender to avoid incorporating strange-looking numbers.*

Finally, the system uses a shorthand in which a double pound sign
(##) shows the start of the Subject: line and a single pound sign (#)
shows the start of the message body. Of course, SMS users understand
this shorthand, but the typical user's tendency to skip over symbols
means symbols you want to use can be overlooked.

Here's how our message looks on a typical cell phone:

First Screen:
Baier_Stein_Dire
ct@66.189.47.16
2##$10 off Oil
Change#Free

Second Screen:
coffee! Oil
change protects
your car's
trade-in value.

Third Screen:
Save $10 2day
only.

Note how easy it is to miss the dollar sign ($) at the start of the Subject: line, since the double pound sign seems to combine with it into a single symbol: ##$. This leads us to tip number three: *Don't begin a Subject: line with a symbol.*

This message has already lost much of our pitch by disguising the sender's identity and incorporating an IP number into the From: header. Note how we also lose clarity by the system's truncation of lines at fifteen characters. For wireless messaging, "Baier Stein Direct" should style itself "Baier Stein Dir," or, even better, "Baier Stein."

Note also that we get only four lines per screen. If the user hasn't erased the message before getting to it, we realize a nice effect in having our offer isolated on the third screen. But that was accidental. We need to plan our message on a fifteen-character-by-four-line template so we can exercise some control over the screen breaks.

A little bit of experimentation shows us that the system tries to break the first line at the "at" sign (@). If we can devise an e-mail address that is at or near fourteen characters before the @ and precisely thirteen characters after it, we can force the system to put our Sender: identification on two lines ending precisely with the double pound sign (##) that introduces the Subject line.

To do this, we need to have a domain that is nine or ten characters long (depending on whether our extension is a three-character one (like ".com" or ".org") or a two-character one (like ".tv"). It may not be possible to secure such a domain, or it may not be worthwhile to try to obtain it. But look how neatly it works:

BSDAutoService@
drivewell.com##

Then, if we compose our message with the fifteen-character line length in mind, we can use the screen breaks to our advantage as well:

First Screen:
BSDAutoService@
drivewell.com##
Save $10 on Oil
Change

Second Screen:
2day!#Keep your
car's trade-in
value. Change
the oil every

Third Screen:
3000 mi. $10 off
2day only. Free
coffee!

It could still use some work, perhaps. But it's much clearer than the first version. You can compose and test such messages by sending them to your own cell phone from one of the web-based wireless messaging services.

The fifteen-character line happens to be what we have on our phone, and it may not be a standard, so you can't always get the line breaks you intend. At all hazards, however, you must avoid using words longer than twelve characters in order not to risk line breaks that could garble your message completely.

Note, however, that this message is not truly a conversation. There's no response mechanism. It assumes that you have some sort of relationship and have had conversations already. If so, you could send it in the morning (when people are thinking about coffee) and try to entice the prospect to drive directly to your shop. This probably will work best if your customers know that you have a standing policy of providing free transportation, since presumably they are getting ready for work or on their way when they get the message. In other words, they must already know you.

On the other hand, the message so far is only 143 characters. You can add fifteen characters for a toll-free telephone number with hyphens (and a space after the final exclamation point) and still be under the 160-character of the SMS budget. But note that if you're doing this through a messaging center, some of them impose limits lower than 160 characters. In that case, you might have to make a choice between a telephone number for response and the front-end premium.

Your goal may be immediate response, but the message can still be effective if the prospect delays response, because the phone will store the message until the user actually deletes it. Thus he or she can keep your 800-number by keeping the message.

This certainly is more detail than the average marketer wants to deal with on a daily basis. However, this kind of attention to detail is necessary to make SMS work effectively and profitably. The limitations imposed will lead to either infrequent use or changes in technology that will broaden the potential of its practical applications.

The Wireless Web

When the wireless web was being developed, the favorite examples of its potential for advertising were allergy medicine and weather reports. The user accesses a weather report on the wireless device, such as a PDA or a wireless application protocol or WAP-enabled phone. Depending on the season or even the weather report itself, the forecast might include a sponsorship message. If the report shows a high pollen count, the reasoning goes, it's a good time to remind the user of the availability of allergy medicine.

For the conversation-oriented marketing professional, the whole point of the wireless web is that it enables what is called "mcommerce" (mobile commerce). We don't want to simply provide people with information; we want to provide them with a response mechanism in order to make the sale. It's hard to imagine anyone using a mobile phone or a PDA to buy allergy medicine. But there are products and services people might buy with a wireless device, e.g., software for the device itself, or movie or concert tickets, items, in other words, for which shipping and delivery are not issues.

One recent survey showed that sixteen percent of respondents had web-enabled phones, but fewer than one percent had used them to make a purchase. "While there are millions of mobile users," said one report, "almost none have used mobile phones to make purchases."[2]

A survey of U.S. consumers in June 2000, found thirty-four percent intending to make purchases by mobile phone. But in a 2001 survey, the number had fallen to three percent.[3] Right now, business-to-business operations hold more promise than consumer marketing does. In the foreseeable future, the wireless web will facilitate sales force automation, field service, shipping and receiving, and supply chain tracking. These business needs may well foster the growth of an mcommerce infrastructure.

Notes

1. The Future of Wireless Marketing, Carat Interactive, 2002.
2. Gilda Raczkowski, "Mobile Ecommerce: Focusing on the Future," Nov. 30, 2002.
3. Ibid.

Marketing Conversations in Action

Putting it Together—Integrating Media for Maximum Results

Now that you have an understanding of how to work creatively within each marketing medium, it's time to put together an integrated communications plan. This plan will provide you with the tactical foundation to build and grow the conversation with your customers—and thereby maximize your results. Although many factors will contribute to your finished plan, there are two main approaches to consider. You can build a plan that is driven by your marketing objective. Or, you can build a plan that is driven by your marketing budget.

In the first scenario, it is important to have a quantifiable goal already articulated. So, instead of stating that you want to acquire new customers, you should specify a realistic number or percentage increase. Predict response rates based on your knowledge of industry standards or your own company's history. Then, choose an integrated schedule of communications vehicles that should achieve your objective.

You may want to extend the metaphor of the new marketing conversation as you proceed. Imagine the ongoing dialogue with your prospects and customers. As it moves from general and introductory to more specific and intimate, you can match appropriate media to each phase of the conversation. This might argue for starting with awareness and brand-building options, such as television, and moving into more targeted choices like direct mail.

If your plan will be designed to match an already determined budget, you'll want to reverse-engineer choices that optimize your investment. Chances are, you'll earmark a smaller portion of that budget for awareness and brand-building (the "getting to know you" part of your conversation), then invest more heavily in demand-generating vehicles, such as direct response print, e-mail, or direct mail.

If your budget is constrained, be careful not to spread yourself too thin. You will probably be better served by using a smaller number of media vehicles with more frequency than by dabbling in a broader range of media.

Either way, it is imperative that you create multiple opportunities for testing, learning, and changing course. As an integrated media marketing "conversationalist" you must ensure that you've created a way to measure response at every touchpoint in your interaction with prospects and customers. Your commitment to making each element accountable will help you make the most of your current budget—and invest wisely in the future. We'll discuss testing a little later in this chapter.

Media 101

Here are some basics that can help you quantify and assess the potential of each media channel. Please note, there are many books and courses available on the science of media planning. If you are allocating a significant advertising budget, you will want to work with an ad agency or media buying service to ensure that you make the best choices.

Reach and Frequency In media, the term "reach" refers to the number of unique people who will receive your message. This is an important piece of data, as it correlates directly to the cost of different media options. To use television as an example, networks can charge top dollar for their high-ranking primetime sitcoms because they offer advertisers a way to reach the most people with their spots. Similarly, magazines invest heavily in acquiring subscribers so that they can charge higher advertising rates.

"Frequency" describes how often the targeted audience will receive your message. In traditional advertising, potential success is measured by a combination of reach and frequency. In other words, the more people reached and the more often those people are reached, the more likely that a campaign will be successful.

But, in the world of the new marketing conversation, bigger isn't necessarily better. There are so many more choices available to both advertisers and consumers today that a smaller media buy can also prove to be more effective and efficient. Today's consumer recognizes mass marketing as a message for the masses. He or she is looking for a more individualized experience.

With that said, you'll still want a clear picture of all the numbers involved as you construct your plan. Consider a medium's reach as a factor when you are comparing like media vehicles. And, you will want to consider how many times your message will appear as you allocate your budget dollars.

Cost per Thousand CPM (Cost per Thousand) is a convenient way to compare pricing. When you meet with sales representatives from different media, they can provide you with these numbers.

Response Potential Most advertising can be described as custom manufacturing. There is no guarantee that one ad or direct mail package will generate the same response as any other. But, you can look at your own marketing history as well as the industry standards of different media to make an educated guess.

It is also helpful to project three response scenarios. Base one on the average numbers achieved in the past. Then, create a plan that generates a realistic improvement on those numbers and one that would represent a realistic decline. This will give you "worst case," "best case" and "most likely" numbers with which to budget.

Timing Two perspectives on media timing can be valuable as you work on your plan. First, consider how long it will take to get your message in front of your prospective customer. This can range from hours, to weeks, or even months.

There may be a way to jumpstart your integrated program and your conversation by first utilizing media with a shorter time to market. For example, e-mails can be written and broadcast in a matter of hours. A radio spot can be conceived, written, produced, and on-air within a week, while production of direct mail may take two weeks, and insertion dates for magazines can be six to eight weeks in advance of publication. By staggering your efforts and producing elements concurrently, you can better manage how quickly your conversation begins.

Second, consider how long it will take for you to get feedback or a response once your marketing message is received. Again, this can be within hours in the case of e-mail or months in the case of print advertising. Plot your responses to each contact and you'll probably recognize bell curves. This can help you time secondary and tertiary touchpoints. Ideally, you want your conversation to build momentum. You should strive to maintain interest and activity without redundancy and wasted budget dollars.

The Medium's Sweet Spot From a marketing perspective, different media choices tend to perform better at different things. For example, television is particularly adept at raising awareness and creating an emotional bond. Radio and newspaper advertising convey urgency and timeliness and can be valuable in translating a national brand into a locally relevant one. Direct mail and e-mail communicate on a one-to-one basis and encourage immediate action.

All of these media can play a role in the integrated new marketing conversation.

Of course, you'll want to consider the specific characteristics of your product or service. Is one or another media vehicle more appropriate for it? What has worked in the past? Or, is it worth testing a new way to reach your audience? When WANG ran television spots for their personal computers in the early 1980s, they broke new ground for the high tech industry and B2B marketers. Today, broadcast ads for computers account for hundreds of millions of dollars in network advertising revenue.

At a strategic level, your integrated media conversation is meant to achieve two things: You want to build your brand, and you want to create demand. For many products and services, this can be done simultaneously by utilizing different media options to connect along a spectrum from emotion to promotion.

Your Integrated Media Conversation

We return now to the principles of the new marketing conversation discussed in the first chapters of this book. As you consider and choose media, it's imperative that you do so from your customer's perspective. This exercise is not about impressing shareholders or finding a forum in which your company can brag about its accomplishments. Think back to that dinner party guest we described, who spoke of nothing and nobody but himself. You certainly don't want to be him.

An equivalent in recent advertising history can be found in the dot-coms that spent millions of dollars for ads during the Super Bowl. In many cases, these start-up companies spent more on "one-shot" ads than they had yet earned in revenue. The companies got a lot of attention, but many (if not most) of them are no longer in business. One comes to mind in which hamsters were shot from a cannon. For all the "media buzz" their ad generated at the time, chances are you can't even remember their name today. Right?

Quite simply, the behavior and preferences of your audience must drive your decisions about media, otherwise, you are wasting your money.

Don't go into the process with a bias toward a particular medium. In large consumer campaigns, television usually drives other media. It is generally the biggest investment of time, money, and talent. Instead, let your customer tell you or show you how they want to converse with you.

When it comes to engaging a customer in conversation, all media are not created equal. Each option plays a specific role in the greater integrated media dialogue. And, while this is a new way of thinking, it's really no more complicated than developing a targeted creative strategy.

The first thing you'll want to do is to create a *media persona* for your targeted customer. This will enhance the typical demographic and psychographic profile by outlining what media your customer turns to for what information. Remember, your plan of how to communicate with them—much like your strategy for what to communicate—must be driven by their preferences and behavior.

Where does your prospective customer turn for entertainment and relaxation? Where do they look for information? How—and how often—do they prefer to be contacted? Are they offer-responsive? If so, is their responsiveness tied to particular media? And, once they've researched options and offers, how do they make purchases?

What you want to uncover is how each medium influences customer behavior independently and, more important, how the right mix of media can create loyal customers and brand advocates over time.

Look at historic data and see if you can find a correlation between media choice and results. Design a campaign that enables you to conduct research "in the field" by building media testing into the front end of your communications plan. Third-party market research about your audience can also reveal usage patterns. But, asking at least a subset of your customers is the best place to start. In fact, it's one of the most respectful ways you can initiate your conversation. Customers appreciate companies that ask permission to communicate and then observe the customer's preferences.

The Working Plan

With a clear understanding of your customer's media usage in mind, you're ready to build your first plan. Consider this a "straw man" and start with a longer list of options than you'll need or than you have budget for. Start by evaluating media categories with a simple "Yes" or "No" criteria. Then dig deeper and consider specific choices within each category. From there, you can hone in on the ones that will give you the greatest yield.

Direct Mail Despite the familiar "junk mail" moniker, direct mail remains an excellent option for communicating with prospects and customers on a one-to-one basis. And, as such, direct mail can be the foundation for your new marketing conversation. You can effectively use direct mail as your initial introduction. You can send mail that asks for permission to continue conversing. And, once you've collected data, initial responses, and queries, direct mail can become a highly effective individualized method for ongoing communication.

Your database is your most valuable tool in building and growing profitable conversations with customers. Direct mail offers a way to learn and add to that database, and it affords you the opportunity to make the most of the data you hold. Consider learning more about new production technologies such as variable data printing so that each piece of mail you send can be as relevant to the recipient as possible.

Say "yes" to direct mail if you:

- Have the opportunity to target your message to different segments.
- Want to test creative, pricing, deadlines, or offers.
- Need "real estate" for a more complex message.
- Know a lot about your customers/prospects and can leverage that data to build your proposition.

Say "no" if:

- You aren't able to make a compelling offer.
- You need to establish "big company credibility" or an emotional bond first.
- Your audience is unknown, too large, or too broad-based to cost-efficiently use direct mail.

Telemarketing There has been a great deal of public interest—not to mention new, restrictive legislation—in telemarketing over the past year. Why all the interest? One reason is that many unscrupulous companies have abused telemarketing. But, the more relevant reason for our discussion is that telemarketing *works*.

Say "yes" to telemarketing if:

- You are communicating with current customers.
- Your message can be positioned (and, more important, believed) as a "service" or "courtesy."
- Your proposition depends on a personal connection and may require iterative dialogue and explanation.

Say "no" to telemarketing if you:

- Are looking for an effective means of prospecting or lead generation.
- Have not invested in systems and technology to ensure that you adhere to state and federal "do-not-call" regulations.

Radio Radio, like television, is adept at creating emotion. But, radio gives you a greater opportunity to target your audience and can be implemented with a much smaller investment. Radio also gives you a chance to start a conversation with your customer in a very intimate setting—often, in their car. Because of this, customers don't usually have as many psychological filters working to block your message. Radio can be a very effective choice for marketers who need to communicate their brand at the local level. Also, radio works particularly well for impulse buys, such as low-ticket retail or fast food.

Say "yes" to radio if:

- Your schedule is aggressive. Radio can be produced and on-air within days.
- Your message is simple and can be absorbed quickly—and retained.
- You have a clear idea of who you are talking to and what station they would listen to.

Say "no" to radio if:

- Your features and benefits need a lot of explanation.
- You must rely on graphics, photographs or visuals to get your message across.
- Your product or service is a "considered purchase," requiring research and informed comparison-shopping.

Television Television is usually considered the sexiest marketing medium, and, in general, no other option gives you the same opportunity to make an impact or create "a buzz." Television spots can build an emotional connection between customer and company. It's a fuller sensory experience than other media—combining sight and sound.

And television commercials give you a chance to educate or entertain, or do both concurrently.

But, television is by far the most expensive category of media to purchase or to produce. Generally speaking, budgets can easily start in the hundreds of thousands to million-dollar range for a national spot. And, even without considering the expenses involved, television is not right for all marketers.

Say "yes" to television if:

- You have a very healthy budget.
- Your product or service appeals to a broad-based audience.
- You need to demonstrate your product in order to sell it.
- You want to make a big announcement.
- Emotion is more important than promotion at this point in your conversation.

Say "no" to television if:

- You are talking to a small or highly specialized audience.
- You need immediate results and action.
- Your budget is limited.

Newsletters Informative vehicles like newsletters make sense for many marketers committed to building a conversation with their customers. Through vehicles like newsletters, booklets, or web sites, you can provide content that your customers will appreciate. By doing so, you give them a reason to continue talking—and listening—to you.

Once you've offered a newsletter to your customers and prospects, it's important to stay true to their perception of it. If they've requested a newsletter about baking, don't send them an eight-page ad for your brand of cake mix. Do some research and make sure that the subjects you do cover are interesting and valuable to your customer.

Say "yes" to a newsletter if:

- There's a natural fit between your product and the newsletter's content.
- You can commit time and budget to an ongoing project.

Say "no" if:

- Your product or service is a commodity or a low-interest category.
- The nature of your product is such that repeat purchases are rare.

Print Like radio, newspaper is a great way to bring a national brand to the local level. When a person is reading the newspaper, they are looking for facts, not fiction; information, not opinions. Carry this through in your newspaper advertising.

Say "yes" to newspaper advertising if:

- You are trying to target an audience segment by geography.
- Your message is immediate, newsworthy, and particularly timely.
- Credibility is key to your message.
- You have an offer they can't refuse.

Say "no" if:

- Your ad needs an extended shelf-life to be effective.
- You need high quality graphics or photography to sell your product.
- Your proposition is similar to the competition's.

Glossy, consumer magazines offer a great way to build your product's personality. These publications have invested years in building their brand and their relationship with their readers. And many of these readers buy the magazine as much for the advertising as for the editorial. For certain high-profile categories, such as fashion and automotive, magazine advertising is a great way to connect with prospective customers.

On the other hand, a countless number of trade and special-interest publications enable marketers to target virtually any profession, community, or hobby.

Say "yes" to magazine advertising if:

- You are looking for longer shelf-life than you could achieve with newspaper.

- Your product will be best served with high-quality graphic treatment.
- You want to communicate an image-based message.
- You find a publication whose readership closely matches your audience.

Say "no" if:

- You are on a tight time frame.
- You are promoting a time-sensitive offer with a looming expiration date.

E-mail As with display advertising on the web, marketers also have become disillusioned with e-mail. When compared to direct mail, e-mail offers time and money savings that made it very attractive to marketers. So attractive, unfortunately, that e-mail in-boxes became overcrowded, and all marketing messages were labeled "Spam." Internet service providers now offer Spam blocking to their members which may filter some of your marketing messages. Of more concern is the recent move to regulate unsolicited e-mail. The recent "Can Spam" legislation calls for a full disclosure approach to e-mail marketing. For example, marketers are prohibited from harvesting e-mail addresses from web sites. Return e-mail addresses must be easy to find and recognize. Subject lines must disclose the commercial purpose of the e-mail message. These regulations are still evolving, so be sure that you and your strategic partners understand the most current legislation when you're ready to launch a campaign.

Otherwise, you may risk a fine, lawsuits and/or alienating your customers.

With that said, e-mail can still play an important role in the total conversation. It is critical though that you understand your customers' preferences and commit to adhering to them.

Say "yes" to e-mail if:

- You are communicating with existing customers.
- You have a well-articulated "opt-in" policy.
- Your offer can be effectively—and succinctly—communicated online.

Say "no" to e-mail if:

- Your prospects (or, in some cases, your customers) don't recognize your company.
- Your customers aren't active e-mail users.
- You are selling anything that might be considered sensitive.

Web Just a few years ago, the web was hailed as the industry's next frontier, as a cure-all for diminishing returns on more traditional advertising vehicles. Then, enthusiasm waned. Click-through rates dramatically declined. Savvy consumers have even invested in technology that enables them to block online ads.

Disappointing for marketers. But, the medium was originally touted as a stand-alone vehicle. If, instead, you adhere to the concept of the new media conversation, the web can add to and enhance the integrated media experience for your prospects and customers. You might choose to sponsor a site or online publication that appeals to your customer, or run an online campaign that complements your offline media.

Say "yes" to web advertising if:

- You can target your audience by interest or affinity.
- Your customers are comfortable with and actively using technology.
- You have opportunities to partner with appropriate online content providers.
- You want to take advantage of multimedia graphics and interactivity.

Say "no" to web advertising if:

- Your product or service is a lower-ticket item or an impulse buy.
- Your customers don't use the Internet.
- You can't segment or target your audience.
- Your budget restraints would require that the medium directly "pay for itself."

Wireless New technologies, such as wireless communications, offer advertisers the chance to be the "first one on their block" when it comes to making an impact with their customers or prospects. This can result in an artificial boost in response, which will decline over time as the novelty wears off and as other advertisers catch on.

If you're considering investing in a new media technology, do so in a controlled way. Test first and give yourself an option to rollout your campaign to a greater audience if the test proves successful.

Say "yes" to new media communications if:

- You are certain that your audience can/will receive your message.
- You aren't blinded by novelty. Use the same ROI criteria you would use for a more traditional option.
- There's a logical connection between the medium and your message that your customer will recognize.

Say "no" if:

- Your audience can't be reached via the medium you're considering.
- You need graphics or emotional elements to sell your message and product.

Focus on the Best. Test the Rest.

Once you have generated a list of potential media options, take out your red pen and start editing. There's no one way to hone in on the best plan. Most likely, you'll use a combination of quantifiable data and more subjective hunches.

Try immersing yourself in the media you're considering. Listen to the radio stations on your list; read back issues of publications; opt-in to similar online communications programs. And, watch for competitive advertising; it can be an interesting exercise. On the one hand, if your competition is investing significant dollars in a particular medium, it's probably working. On the other hand, unless you have a distinctive selling proposition, your message may get confused with that of the competition.

Once you have a shorter list of potential choices, you can also call sales representatives and ask for proposals. Media reps are notoriously aggressive, so take advantage of all they know, but don't relinquish your control. Ask for very specific examples of successful campaigns. And don't hesitate to ask for clarification if the data you get from one media rep contradicts data you've received from his or her competition.

Budgeting Your Conversation

By now, you've probably amassed a number of media vehicles with which to converse with your customers and prospects. Again, there is no one definitive way to allocate your budget dollars. However, when you focus on the ideal of an ongoing integrated media conversation, several principles emerge to guide you.

Budget by Response Potential This is where the historical data and industry norms we referenced earlier become valuable. Too often, companies dedicate an inordinately large part of their budget to one-way communication. This is talking at your customers, not with them. A better use of your budget is to apportion it based on the potential yield of each media contact. If most of your leads or sales are coming in through print advertising, invest accordingly.

Determine which media vehicles are necessary at a maintenance level. Some presence on television or in consumer magazines, for example, may need to be sustained in order to keep your quality brand top of mind. But, if direct mail and e-mail are generating most of your leads, consider allocating a good portion or even most of your budget to them.

Even without historical data to work with, this method can be easily tested, and benchmarks can be set. Test each media vehicle early on and then use the comparative results to determine media spending for the rest of your campaign.

Budget by the Flow of Your Conversation This approach is based less on numbers and more on your understanding of the sales cycle of your product. Map out a typical sales cycle, moving your hypothetical prospect from needs assessment, through awareness, consideration, narrowing their options, and eventually purchase. You can go further and include repeat purchases for current customers as well. Now, budget according to the amount of time and attention the prospect will spend at each phase.

A similar approach, which may be more appropriate for some marketers, is to define the stages of the marketing conversation. These may include introductions, establishing interest, engaging in a back-and-forth of ideas, final considerations, and then a purchase (the end of their first conversation with you and, perhaps, the start of the next one). Use these stages, their timing and importance, to help you allocate your budget.

Budget by the Customer's Perceived Value of the Contact Today's customers are more aware of companies' marketing efforts than ever before, and many recognize the expense and effort that goes into the advertising they receive. These same customers appreciate marketers who listen to, and invest in, what matters to them. So, an ad that appears self-serving and clearly costs a lot to produce will not just fail. It can actually alienate a potential customer.

In a way, this is the simplest approach to thinking about your media communications budget. Consider each marketing contact and ask yourself if it matters to your customer. Will it encourage them to stay in their conversation with you? If it does, invest more in it. If not, invest less. Or think about whether you should cut it completely.

A Few Strong Words about Testing

There's no exact science to planning media. And there's no one right way for you to build your integrated media program. The first plan you put together will be your "best guess" and, certainly, should not be considered final. That's why your commitment to testing is so important.

Testing is how you enable your customers to take an active role in the conversation. It allows them to tell you what matters to them and what doesn't. As direct marketers, we cannot overemphasize the importance of testing. The overall mix, sequence, and timing of conversational touchpoints can and should be efficiently tested and fine-tuned. We recommend using an iterative testing model—testing in waves to determine a winner or "control" at each stage. In this way, you'll continually learn and see improvement. You'll want to test each individual medium—categorically and specifically. You should also continually test your messaging, communication sequences, offers, and timing. And, you should also build tests that determine how your media selections interact and how they affect response vehicles. For example, newspaper ads may increase visits to your web site, while radio ads may increase inbound calls, or vice versa. There's no way to know without testing.

Summary

There's an expression in marketing that you should "Fish where the fish are." But, for your new marketing conversation to be fruitful, where they are can't be your only consideration. What are they doing while they are there? Any media sales rep can give you demographics of their medium's audience (although, you should approach these with an entire shaker's worth of salt). To move into conversation territory, you need an understanding of your customer's receptiveness to your message while they're there.

When someone sits down to watch television after a day at work, they are not comparison-shopping. They are looking to be entertained, to laugh or cry, and to feel relaxed. That's why television is a good medium with which to build a brand. Conversely, a customer who reads the newspaper is looking for information. Give them facts and timely offers. A prospect who is reviewing his or her e-mail or emptying a mailbox is looking for personal and relevant communication.

Remember, you need to know who your customer is—and how they can be and want to be reached in order to use integrated marketing media to your advantage.

Action Plan for Building Your New Marketing Conversation

A decade ago, there was a shift in thought to "relationship marketing," which was an early effort to use multiple media in order to build a relationship between buyers and sellers. Today's marketers are taking that concept a step further by taking into account the customer's needs and preferences, and allowing that information to drive individualized and seamlessly woven, integrated media marketing.

This approach is paying off. Whether your customers understand the process or not, if you establish and maintain an integrated media conversation with them, your sales, brand loyalty, and customer retention will improve.

Consumers don't recognize all the mechanics of a successful marketing conversation. They do notice, however, when the conversations they have with companies break down. Here are just a handful of common disconnects. If you haven't experienced them as a marketer, you surely will be familiar with them as a consumer.

Multiple Personalities

You receive an offer in the mail that sounds pretty good. You're tempted, but being a typical consumer, you're wary of marketing offers from companies you've never heard of. So, the mail ends up in the trash. The thing is, you actually do know the company. They advertise regularly on your favorite television show. They have billboards on the road you drive to work each day. In fact, you've bought from them in the past. So what happened?

The company trying to sell to you has different marketing managers charged with utilization of each medium. Each of these managers uses different agencies to develop and execute their campaigns. Each of these agencies has a separate creative team that's doing great work for their client. However, no one is looking at the big picture. The result is a fragmented conversation and a lot of missed opportunity.

Nobody's Listening

You call the toll-free number of a company you already do business with. You have a billing or customer service issue you need to discuss with someone. While you're on hold, a recorded message asks you to key in your twelve-digit account number so that they may service your request more quickly. You do. After a few minutes wait, a service representative gets on the line. What's the first question he or she asks? "What's your account number?"

Do you protest that you've already given it to them? Suggest they invest in telephony systems that can actually talk to each other? Or, do you sigh, shrug, and repeat the number to the rep? Chances are, it isn't worth your time to complain, but your satisfaction with that company just decreased.

Strangers are Treated Better than Loyal Customers

You've subscribed to a publication for years. When it's time to renew, you receive an offer for twenty-five percent off the cover price. You would appreciate this if it weren't for one thing. BRCs that have been blown in to the magazine itself offer fifty percent off, but the sweeter offer is only available to new customers. The reward for your loyalty to the publication? A higher price.

This is an example of the common practice of investing heavily in attaining new customers while letting current customers lapse. How would you feel if you were engaged in a conversation and the other person abruptly stopped listening, and went to talk to someone else? Marketers do this all the time.

Again, Nobody's Listening

You purchase something on the web and complete an online form with your billing and shipping information. They ask for your e-mail in order to process the order. Directly beneath that field, you can request not to receive e-mail solicitations, and you do so. However, shortly after submitting your order, you begin to get e-mails from the seller. When you call or e-mail to complain, you learn that it takes four to six weeks for your opt-out to be entered in the system.

There are reasons for all of these disconnects—operational issues, antiquated systems, silos within the organization. Over time, however, customers who experience these frustrations will be lost to other companies that know how to build and maintain an integrated conversation.

Hard Work But Worth It

Holding up your end of the new marketing conversation is hard work. By its very nature, a conversation with your customer must be dynamic. As his or her interests and needs evolve, the conversation must evolve as well. This makes it difficult to rest on your laurels or to repeat programs and campaigns because they've served you well in the past. In a marketing conversation, each prospect or customer is treated as an individual with unique and ever changing communication requirements.

Your job is made more difficult since a commitment to leveraging the principles of ongoing customer conversation has to be shared by multiple stakeholders in your company. In other words, the focus on the customer can't start with marketing communications. It has to be a more holistic attitudinal shift. It has to start with your product or service. Are you selling something you make or are you providing something the customer needs?

Operations must be brought into the picture. The most sophisticated marketing relationship can be undermined easily when the company's billing system doesn't talk to the CRM system being used by customer service. To complicate the situation, sales is going in one direction while marketing is going in another.

Silos in companies make it difficult to live up to the customer's idea of a relationship. Different functional groups often have their own agendas, their own objectives, and their own budgets. Some forward-thinking companies resolve this dilemma by creating new positions, such as Vice President of Customer Experience, with authority across traditionally discreet functions and departments.

If, as a marketer, you are trying to refocus and integrate your programs, take the time to win over the other teams in your own company first. Involve sales in developing and articulating your message. Check with customer-facing personnel, such as service reps, to ensure that your messaging fits what they've heard and will resonate with customers. Work closely with billing, operations, and IT so that your conversation doesn't disconnect at key moments, such as purchase or delivery.

One approach might be to create a task force with delegates from all departments or functions that relate to the customer. This way, each team's objectives and operational issues will be represented as you work towards a unified set of customer experience goals.

Remember, your customer doesn't know or care that marketing, sales, manufacturing, service, and billing work out of five different locations and see each other only once a year at the company picnic.

Similarly, many marketers run into obstacles when components of the overall program are developed by different outside vendors and resources. Earlier, we advised that you approach your program with media neutrality. You must also refrain from allowing one outside partner to dictate a strategy that is too myopic. An ad agency will naturally suggest a strategy appropriate to advertising, a direct marketing firm will have a similar bias toward direct marketing, and your P.R. firm will expect public relations to solve any and all of your problems.

One solution is to use a single outside partner for everything, though this can be quite costly and unrealistic since most agencies have weaknesses as well as strengths. You may be better served with several relationships, as long as you can create and maintain a true team-based solution.

If possible, include strategists from each of these outside partners in your planning. Select organizations that are best-of-breed in their specific discipline and ask for senior-level contributors for this critical first stage. Once your interdisciplinary team has agreed to and articulated one shared communications strategy, you'll find it easier to manage project teams. Keep in mind that no matter how many agency people you gather at your strategy sessions, the most important contributor to the process must be your customer. We return to the basics: What do they want? What do they need? How, when, and in what way do they want you to communicate with them?

Tell Us What You Want

For your new marketing conversation to work, you must use any and all the knowledge you have about the customer to start the dialogue, and then commit to dynamic, two-way communication going forward. Your conversation can't occur once a quarter in a discreet direct mail package. It needs to be an ongoing conversation throughout the year and throughout your relationship with each and every customer. There are several ways to gather the information you need to build conversations with your customers.

Focus Groups Budget permitting, focus groups should be scheduled continually and not just when a specific campaign is being launched. If a conversation is to evolve, your customers' opinions, feelings, and preferences should be gauged frequently and cumulatively.

Internal Focus Groups Who within your organization is closest to the customer? Is it sales or customer service? Schedule frequent sessions in which these internal teams can share their learning with teams that are further removed from the customer. Think of the value this "insider information" can offer R&D, marketing, or manufacturing.

Surveys Commit to surveying your customers on a regular basis. Specific timing depends on the nature of your product or service and the profile of your customer. Plan to survey infrequently enough that response stays high but often enough to course correct if you learn that your overall conversation is off-track. People appreciate the opportunity to give their input. In many cases, a straightforward survey will out-pull a higher cost package with graphics and clever copy.

Opinions Ask for customer opinions on everything from your marketing materials, customer service, and operations to the product itself. People want to be heard. Be sure to acknowledge their contribution and, whenever appropriate, act upon it.

Suggestion Boxes Even in this day of e-mail, voice-mail, and other technology, many companies still post suggestion boxes in lunchrooms and common areas and employees still stuff those boxes with everything from ideas for the holiday party to mission-critical business improvements. These boxes are still popular precisely because they are so low-tech. It's a no-brainer, there's no commitment, and no paper trail. Set up the same kind of device on your web site or through other media. Don't insist that customers tell you who they are; just give them a no-strings-attached way to talk to you.

Telemarketing As we've mentioned earlier, telemarketing as an industry and a communications method has had some very bad press lately. But, outbound telemarketing is still an effective and relatively cost-efficient way to meet your customers one-on-one. Try using telemarketing to get information and feedback from current customers rather than using it as a sales tool. Following up after a purchase to ensure that the customer is satisfied gives you a way to get some valuable learning while reinforcing the customer's value to your organization.

Package Inserts Many companies spend a large sum on packing and shipping their products. Take advantage of those set costs and use them for marketing purposes. Never send a product out to a customer without asking for their opinion, feedback, and suggestions.

Statement Stuffers Similarly, if you're in a business that sends periodic bills or statements, make the most of all the postage you're paying. A quick survey or simple reply card can be created and inserted for pennies.

The marketing organization that boasts that it received a twenty percent response to a customer service survey is missing the point. Getting input is not the goal. Your mission is to use any and all input you receive to direct your marketing communications. The option to talk to you—to converse—must be present at every customer touchpoint.

How Do You Get Them to Tell You What They Want?

Privacy has become a central and sensitive topic these days. Consumers are wary of releasing any information about themselves, their buying habits, or even their personal preferences. So how do you get customers to raise their hands if and when they have something to say?

The trick is to use the "Two Rs:" rationale and reward. Explain, in straightforward language, your rationale. Why you are asking for the information? Is it to improve your systems? Are you trying to better understand and respond to their needs? Are you working to lower your operational costs and pass on the savings to customers? Think of ways to word your request in copy so that your customer understands why they should cooperate. Some examples follow.

- In order to expedite future orders, can you please provide the following . . .
- We're listening. Please tell us about your experience so we can ensure your satisfaction in the future.
- Our new statements will lower costs for all our customers, but we need your help to make it work.

The second "R" is reward. Offers have always been an important key to the success of marketing. In the case of asking for personal data, adding a reward is more important than ever before. Consumers recognize that their information is valuable to companies that want to do business with them and many won't be willing to release it without some compensation. Consider offering a discount, a gift certificate, a premium item, VIP customer status, or some other form of preferential treatment as an incentive.

Go Ahead, Start a Conversation

Time has become an invaluable commodity. Everyone feels rushed, frazzled, and pulled in too many different directions. Consumers in virtually every category are responding to this by tuning out marketing messages.

The best way to capture and keep their attention is to engage them in a marketing conversation—an integrated media dialogue driven by their requests, responses, and preferences.

Going forward, the best use of marketing media will be to surround your prospects and customers with an interwoven set of messages that are appropriate both to the strengths of each medium and, especially, to the needs and interests each customer has expressed.

The word "conversation" isn't part of your customers' vernacular when they think about your company, your product, or service. That's okay. With a commitment to listening, with the right media tools and marketing message, you can successfully engage customers.

Listen to your customers and build their needs and preferences into your strategic plan. Use individual media vehicles in the way they work best, to build awareness, urgency, affinity, or community. Use a total integrated media approach to surround them with a tapestry of relevant messages. Don't give customers one size fits all when they're asking for haute couture. You have to custom tailor your communications to their unique needs, requests, and behavior.

We encourage you to become your own organization's champion for the new marketing conversation. Your customers will thank you for it. They'll thank you with dollars.

Audience Media Profile

Project:

Date:

Project Manager:

MEDIA HABITS
Describe a "day in the life" of your prospect or customer. With what media does he or she interact during the course of the day?

Morning:

Afternoon:

Evening:

STATED MEDIA PREFERENCES
Via what communications vehicle(s) has your audience requested to receive information?

MEDIA BEHAVIOR
What media does your audience turn to for the following types of content? List media channels and any specifics you have.

Entertainment:

Education:

Product Research:

Product Purchase:

Business Information:

Personal/Family/Home Information:

Creative Strategy Brief

Project:

Date:

Project Manager:

SITUATION ANALYSIS
In this section, describe the current market for the product or service and specifics about the company, as it relates to the competition. Who are the other players in your space? What are their offerings? And, more importantly, how are they communicating with customers?

MARKETING OBJECTIVES
List primary and secondary objectives. Be as focused—and specific—as you can.

PRODUCT/SERVICE OVERVIEW
What are the features and benefits of your product or service?

AUDIENCE AND ITS NEEDS
Describe your audience with as much detail and "color commentary" as you have access to.

CURRENT AND DESIRED BEHAVIOR
This section comprises a description of what your prospective customer is doing today, and what you want them to do once they receive your marketing message.

VALUE PROPOSITION

If your audience purchases your product or service, what will they receive or accomplish?

OBSTACLES AND BRIDGES

What perceptions or realities may keep your audience from responding? What can you promote to bridge these obstacles?

STRATEGY

How will your campaign be constructed? What media will you use? What formats? How often will you communicate with your audience and in what sequence? What offers can you make at each touchpoint?

CREATIVE GUIDELINES

List or refer your team to any corporate identity standards or previous campaigns that must be referenced to develop the new program.

TIMING, "NEXT STEPS" AND MILESTONES

Insert a project timeline and assign scheduled responsibilities to team members. If there are media or production deadlines, list them here as well.

Media Checklist

Project:

Date:

Project Manager:

MEDIA CHECKLIST
As a first step to developing your working plan, select or eliminate media vehicles based on this simple checklist.

[ ] **Direct Mail**

Do you have the opportunity to target your message to different
segments?

Do you want to test creative, pricing, deadlines or offers?

Do you need "real estate" for a more complex message?

Do you know a lot about your customers/prospects and can leverage
that data to build your proposition?

[ ] **Television**

Do you have a very healthy budget?

Does your product or service appeal to a broad-based audience?

Do you need to demonstrate your product in order to sell it?

Do you want to make a big announcement?

Is emotion more important than promotion at this point in your
conversation?

[ ] **Radio**

Is your schedule aggressive?

Is your message simple, quickly absorbed and retained?

Do you have a clear idea of who you are talking to—and what station
they listen to?

[ ] **Telemarketing**

Are you communicating with current customers?

Can your message be positioned and believed as a "service" or
"courtesy?"

Does your proposition depend on a personal connection and require iterative dialogue and explanation?

[ ] **Web Advertising**

Can you target your audience by interest or affinity?

Are your customers comfortable with using technology?

Do you have opportunities to partner with appropriate online content providers?

Can you take advantage of multimedia graphics and interactivity?

[ ] **E-mail**

Are you communicating with existing customers?

Do you have a well-articulated "opt-in" policy?

Can your offer be effectively and succinctly communicated online?

[ ] **Newspaper Advertising**

Are you trying to target your audience segment by geography?

Is your message immediate, newsworthy and particularly timely?

Is credibility key to your message?

Do you have an offer they can't refuse?

[ ] **Magazine Advertising**

Are you looking for longer shelf-life?

Will your message benefit from high quality graphics?

Do you want to communicate an image-based message?

Can you find a publication whose readership closely matches your audience?

[ ] **Wireless**

Are you certain your audience can/will receive your message?

Does it make sense from an ROI perspective?

Is there a logical connection between the medium and your message?

[ ] **Newsletter**

Is there a natural fit between your product and the newsletter's content?

Can you commit time and budget to an ongoing project?

Offer Checklist

Project:

Date:

Project Manager:

PURPOSE OF OFFER
What is the objective? What action should your offer motivate?

[ ]   Register

[ ]   Request more information

[ ]   Visit a retail location

[ ]   Trial

[ ]   Place a first order

[ ]   Make a repeat purchase

[ ]   Renew a subscription or membership

[ ]   Refer someone

[ ]   Other _____

QUALIFICATION
Are you looking for highly qualified leads or a high quantity of responses? Indicate along the continuum below.

■ ─────────────────────────────────────── ■

High Quality   High Quantity

POTENTIAL OFFERS

The list below is ranked from highest quantity response (at top of list) to highest quality response (bottom of list).

[ ]   Premium items and free gifts

[ ]   Sweepstakes

[ ]   Contests (of skill)

[ ]   Free information about category

[ ]   Information kits

[ ]   Case histories/true customer stories

[ ]   Free information about the product or service

[ ]   Registering for a mailing (or e-mailing) list

[ ]   Free trial

[ ]   Free estimate

[ ]   In-person or telephone sales call

OFFER CRITERIA

Once you have an offer in mind, rank it against other offers, using the following criteria.

[ ]   Relevant to prospective customer?

[ ]   Relevant to your product or service?

[ ]   Projected ROI?

[ ]   Unique?

[ ]   Does it encourage a continuing conversation?

[ ]   Other: _____

Testing Worksheet

Project:

Date:

Project Manager:

VARIABLES TO BE TESTED
Tests are most informative when they focus on single elements of your campaign, such as:

[ ] Offer

[ ] Media vehicle

[ ] List

[ ] Creative

[ ] Timing

[ ] Other: _____

OBJECTIVE
What is the objective and what results do you want to measure to achieve it?

STRUCTURE OF TEST
How many cells will you be testing? (If you are testing multiple variables, keep cells discrete—test only one variable in each cell.)

TESTING "TREE"

Test in phases or waves, in order to apply learning as efficiently as possible. As in a "round-robin" tennis tournament, you can use this worksheet as winning campaigns emerge.

_____

Winning Campaign or "Control"

_____   _____

Winner Phase 2   Phase 3 Test

_____ _____ _____

Winner Phase 1   Phase 2, Test 1   Phase 2, Test 2

_____ _____ _____

Phase 1, Test 1   Phase 1, Test 2   Phase 1, Test 3

DIRECTIONS: Start at the lowest level (Phase 1) of the tree and test multiple solutions. After each testing Phase is completed, move the winning solution up a level and test it against new solutions. In this example, we've indicated three phases of testing, but your objectives and budget may dictate more or less. Upon completion, a winning "control" will be determined and can be rolled out to a greater universe of prospective customers.

Case Studies

Conversations in Action: Bogdon Candy

The niceties added to a customer's experience can make the difference when it comes to satisfaction and loyalty. In fact, sometimes that extra touch means more to a customer than the core product or service.

A perfect example of this can be found in a sub-segment of the food services industry: after-dinner confections. Just ask the Bogdon Candy Company or their direct marketing agency Hogan & Associates.

Situation

The Bogdon Candy Company is a family-owned business, with over three generations making fine confections in the same way they did more than fifty years ago, over an open fire, in only one hundred-pound batches at a time. Today, Bogdon, located in Kansas City, Missouri, makes, sells, and ships more than one hundred million "Reception Sticks" every year.

Bogdon's "Reception Sticks" and "Mint Double-Dips" are described as "The ultimate after-dinner chocolate. These candies are a scrumptiously refreshing "surprise" consisting of a delectable fruit or a refreshing mint coated with exquisite, rich, dark chocolate." Each candy is individually wrapped and usually bears the name of the restaurant serving it.

Over the years, Bogdon candies have received many prestigious awards, including "Best Domestic Candy" from the National Association of Specialty Food Trade and "Best Domestic Candy" from the International Fancy Food Administration.

However, regardless of Bogdon's quality and reputation, the econ-

All information, including all illustration, is reprinted with permission of the Bogdon Candy Co.

omy has affected new business efforts. Restaurant owners and managers, like professionals in most business categories, are under pressure to reduce costs and increase profits. So, it's no surprise that the after-dinner confections most commonly presented with the check or left in the maitre d's reception area are plain, plastic-wrapped mints. Most of these are purchased through food brokerages.

By comparison, Bogdon's "Reception Sticks" and "Mint Double-Dips" are more costly for restaurateurs. Bogdon was convinced, however, that they provide a distinctive, finishing touch to their customers' fine dining experience.

The challenge was to use a modest direct marketing budget to convince the target audience as well.

Marketing Objectives

The main objectives were to generate qualified leads, obtain new customers, and ultimately increase sales of both Bogdon "Reception Sticks" and "Double Dip Mints." Although product trial would be encouraged, it was more important to build a long-term relationship. The average new Bogdon customer costs the company money the first year. However, lifetime value increases rapidly as a customer makes repeat purchases in years two, three, four and five. (A chart with actual assigned values follows the results section of this case study.)

In order to achieve this goal, the marketing program had to increase the awareness of Bogdon's products. The communications had to provide the rationale for restaurateurs to pay more for a quality after-dinner candy that aligns better with their restaurant's desired dining experience. Since this target audience had many responsibilities, the program needed to make it as easy as possible for them to order customized Bogdon products.

Target Audience

The audience consisted of owners and managers of high-end "white tablecloth" restaurants and chains. The good news was that the audience was pre-disposed to prefer Bogdon's products. In fact, based on findings from a Gallup study, discerning restaurant owners and managers realized that seventy-two percent of their customers occasionally or always eat an after-dinner mint. Sixty-eight percent of their customers prefer individually wrapped mints. Fifty-two percent of their customers who eat out often, in other words, their best customers, preferred a chocolate mint rather than a regular mint.

Budget continued to be a driver. According to the National Restaurant Association, more than seven out of ten eating-and-drinking places are single-unit (independent) operations, and one out of three eating-and-drinking places is a sole proprietorship or partnership. These hands-on decision-makers were faced with countless choices about operating expenses on a daily basis.

Challenges

Bogdon had a modest budget, which would limit the media and the number of touchpoints they would be able to implement. It would also limit the number of response mechanisms that could be deployed.

The category was low interest. Despite the Gallup study, the finer quality after-dinner mints were considered a "nice-to-have," not a "need-to-have." The marketing conversation had to change this perception.

Strategy

To reach the target audience, the Bogdon Candy Company incorporated postcard direct mail for lead generation, three-dimensional fulfillment mail packages, inbound telemarketing, and the company's web site.

In most cases, envelope packages traditionally out-pull postcards. But, for this campaign, Hogan felt comfortable recommending more cost-efficient postcards. Because of the nature of their business, owners and managers of restaurants are typically referred to as a "stand-up" audience (people who spend most of their working hours moving about) versus a "sit-down" audience (people who spend most of their working hours at a desk). As a result, the former is more receptive to self-mailer formats, while the latter is more receptive to personalized, closed-face envelope mailings.

The rationale behind the program was to send a series of attention-getting, highly personalized direct mail pieces that would illustrate the product with great impact. Through high-resolution digital printing, each postcard demonstrated the customized "Reception Sticks" with the individual restaurant's name printed on the product. Personalization was also incorporated into the headline and throughout the body copy. A series of postcards was mailed one week apart for greatest impact and continuity.

Samples of after dinner confections were offered to respondents. This enabled the prospect to experience the quality of Bogdon products for themselves with a free sample box of "Reception Sticks" and "Double Dip Mints." The fulfillment package included a personalized letter and an order form for respondents to use in placing their first order.

The fulfillment package also promoted special introductory offers, designed to encourage retention and continuity. When the prospect placed their first order, they had a choice of receiving one free case for every three cases ordered or a free printing plate to engrave their restaurant's name and logo on the candy wrappers. This offer, in particular was designed to foster a long-term relationship.

Messaging

As mentioned earlier, one of the biggest hurdles Bogdon faced was convincing people to spend more money on an expense, which was not perceived to be a necessity. This would prove to be the most important part of the communications stream or conversation. The most appropriate place to discuss this was the fulfillment package.

The letter, copywritten by Earl Hogan, does an excellent job educating the prospect about the value of their brand. Note the conversational tone of the following passages

> *By enhancing your brand's equity, you keep customers coming back. In turn, they tell their friends and families about your restaurant. In his best-selling business book,* The Anatomy of Buzz—How to Create Word-of-Mouth Marketing, *author Emanuel Rosen tells us that friends and relatives are the Number One source of information about places to visit.*
>
> *That's why it's so important—from entering to leaving—that attention to every detail of making your customers' "total Dining Experience" more memorable than your competitors' is what will ensure their return.*

The copy continues by making a direct case for paying more for Bogdon's products.

Paying a few pennies more for a high quality confection that expresses greater gratitude than what your guests may be accustomed to receiving at other dining establishments can make a significant difference in their minds—especially when preparing to leave. And each time, you're enhancing your brand's equity.

If a prospect went to Bogdon's web site, they encountered the same tone of voice as they learned more about the history of the company and the quality of its products.

The messaging throughout all the conversational touches reinforced the idea that after-dinner mints should not be considered a commodity item.

Implementation

The total mailing file consisted of 4,892 address records. In order to gauge response and appropriately staff inbound telemarketing lines, a first mailing of five hundred was sent out. The remainder of the list was mailed in one-week intervals.

The production cost per piece, including First Class (presorted) postage, was seventy-six cents each.

As responses were received, respondents were flagged and suppressed in subsequent mailings. Fulfillment packages with samples were sent out the same day the inbound toll-free call was received by Bogdon.

Results

The four-part mailing series generated 411 responses—a cumulative response rate of 11.9%

The number of first-time customers acquired after the fulfillment mailing was forty-eight. This represents better than a ten percent conversion rate.

The number of retained customers—those who ordered a second time—was thirty-eight.

The average order size was six hundred dollars; the average order

Multiple postcards were sent to build awareness and make an impact.

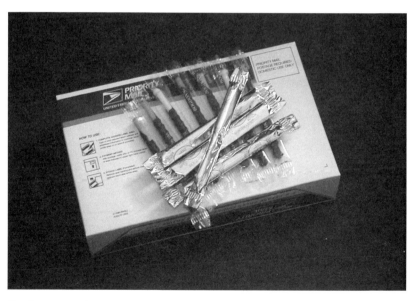

Product samples were sent to respondents via Priority Mail.

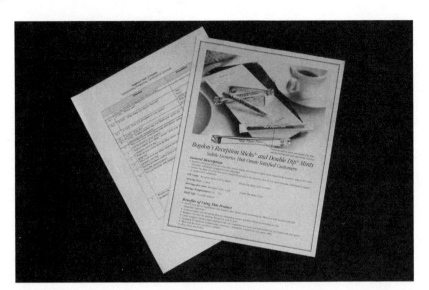

Additional touchpoints included telemarketing and promotional inserts.

Postcards featured a creative use of variable data personalization.

size for second orders placed during the first year was four hundred dollars. Retention from the first to the second year is expected to be eighty percent. Expected lifetime value for each new customer after the second year is expected to be $251. And, after the fifth year, this is expected to reach $1,104, making this marketing conversation a very sweet success story.

	1st Year	2nd Year	3rd Year	4th Year	5th Year
First-Time Buyers	48				
Average Spending Level for First-Time Buyers	$600				
Total Revenue from First-Time Buyers	$28,800				
First-Time Buyers who made subsequent purchases	**38**				
Average Amount of subsequent purchases during 1st Year	$1,000				
Total Revenue from subsequent purchases from First-Time Buyers	$38,000				
Customer retention rate	79%	95%	95%	90%	90%
Number of First-Time Buyers retained as Customers		36	34	33	29
Total Average Annual Revenue from Retained Customers		$1,500	$1,500	$1,500	$1,500
Total Sales Revenue	**$66,800**	**$54,150**	**$51,443**	**$48,870**	**$43,983**
Cost Percent for Fixed and Variable Expenses	80.00%	70.00%	60.00%	60.00%	60.00%
Fixed and Variable Cost	$53,440	$37,905	$30,866	$29,322	$26,390
Total Marketing Cost for Acquisition and Retention	$14,871	$1,354	$1,286	$1,222	$1,100
Total Cost	$68,311	$39,259	$32,152	$30,544	$27,490
Gross Profit	-$1,511	$14,891	$19,291	$18,326	$16,494
Discount Rate	1	0.9091	0.8264	0.7513	0.683
Net Present Value Profit	($1,511)	$13,538	$15,942	$13,769	$11,265
Cumulative Net Present Value Profit	($1,511)	$12,027	$27,969	$41,737	$53,003
Lifetime Customer Value	**-$31**	**$251**	**$583**	**$870**	**$1,104**

Conversations in Action: J. D. Edwards

An important element of any marketing conversation is the marketer's ability to speak the customer's language. In every touchpoint, and in headlines, copy and art, the customer needs to recognize that the marketing company understands both their business and their unique and immediate needs.

The Frantz Group's integrated creative work was able to do just that for client J.D. Edwards.

Situation

J.D. Edwards, a $904 million high technology leader founded in 1977, offers integrated solutions that improve the profitability of its business clients.

The J.D. Edwards Solution for Construction is a comprehensive ebusiness solution that manages financial and operations processes, such as project management, workforce management, enterprise asset management, financial management, and business intelligence. J.D. Edwards has a long history of serving the construction industry, as exemplified in their stellar client list. In fact, approximately one-third of the top one hundred contractors uses J.D. Edwards.

The construction business can be volatile. In order to maintain a competitive advantage, contractors must improve the output of their stretched resources (labor, equipment, subcontractors, material) through improved communications, accurate performance measurement, and integrated processes that increase productivity. Specifically, J.D. Edwards helps these companies improve performance by:

- Reducing direct project costs with *J.D. Edwards Project Management*
- Improving asset utilization with *J.D. Edwards Enterprise Asset Management*
- Improving labor productivity and administration with *J.D. Edwards Workforce Management*

Marketing Objectives

The overall objective was to build a pipeline of approximately twelve million dollars in sales. In order to do this, the integrated marketing campaign had to:

- Generate awareness and preference for J.D. Edwards' solutions
- Communicate J.D. Edwards functionality and expertise within the construction marketplace
- Generate qualified leads, which was most important.

Target Audience

The J.D. Edwards product suite was most appropriate for larger construction companies, ranging in size from one hundred thirty million to two billion dollars.

The targeted audience comprised senior-level decision-makers, including C-Level (CEO, COO, CIO) executives, Vice Presidents, and Directors. These are pragmatic, solution seekers. They are looking for a partner who can solve their business problem rather than re-engineer their entire enterprise.

Strategy

The Frantz Group recommended an integrated media campaign that would utilize print and online advertising, direct mail, e-mail, the web, and inbound and outbound telemarketing. This multimedia blitz aimed to surround the target audience with the message that J.D. Edwards is the best technology partner for the construction industry.

At each touchpoint, prospects were given multiple ways to respond, or join in the conversation. These included dedicated 800-numbers, BRCs, and an interactive microsite.

In order to convey the client's expertise in the construction industry, an offer was developed, encouraging prospects to "Take the J.D. Edwards Construction Challenge." This engaging interactive test, which uncovered how each company stacked up against the competition, appealed to the prospect's competitive nature.

Messaging

There were really two parts to the program's messaging. The integrated media conversation needed to communicate that J.D. Edwards understands and services the construction industry. And, it needed to convey a sense of relevancy and urgency—"We can help you right now."

Fortunately, J.D. Edwards has built much of its corporate messaging around the concept of "listening to customers." The J.D. Edwards web site explains that

> . . . Our aim is to make our customers stronger, enabling them to effectively solve their most important business challenges. We do this by listening to our customers, innovating on their behalf, and delivering solutions as part of a results-oriented relationship based on trust and a culture of service.
>
> Our customers say that they want good functionality, tailored for their industries. They say that they want solutions that work the way they work; start where they want to start; and grow in the direction they want to grow. They say that they want a clearer connection between price and value.
>
> We listen carefully. Then, we incorporate what we hear into new and enhanced software products and services.

This is an excellent example of a company promoting the concept of a dynamic dialogue with customers to its customers. The ongoing conversation is positioned as a customer benefit.

Integrated Media Conversation

In January, 2002, a rich html e-mail was sent to rented e-mail addresses of senior managers within the construction segment. Recipients were introduced to J.D. Edwards solutions. A mini-case study was included to build credibility. The "Construction Challenge" offer drove interested prospects to a linked landing page and questionnaire microsite.

Shortly after the e-mail blast, a full-page, four-color print advertisement began running multiple times in several industry trade publications. These included:

*High-impact
direct mail
included an
engaging
"pop-up."*

*Rich html
emails were sent
to qualified
rented lists.*

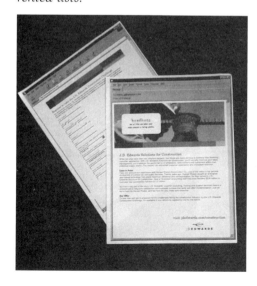

*Print advertising ran
in four targeted trade
publications.*

- *ENR*—The ad ran once a month from February through October, 2002.
- *Constructech*—The ad ran monthly from April through September, 2002.
- *Design Build*—The ad ran in two quarterly issues, March and June, 2003.
- *Sourcebook*—The ad was also placed in this annual industry directory, which was published in June, 2002.

The ad featured a close-up photo of a construction worker. A headline set off against the photo read, "Hardhats are of little use when your problem is falling profits." Speaking to the senior-level executives, this headline achieved two things. It placed J.D. Edwards in the construction industry. And, perhaps more important, it gave the reader a reason to join into the conversation.

Banner advertising also ran concurrently on two complementary web sites:

- *Construction.com*—Banners ran February through April, 2002.
- *ENR.com*—Banners also ran February through April, 2002.

In each case, the viewer was encouraged to test his own company's situation by taking the "J.D. Edwards Construction Challenge."

In March, three months into this multimedia program, a high-impact, three-dimensional direct mail package was sent to the top tiers of the target audience. The package included a custom label, personalized letter tailored to either the C-level or Vice President-level executive, a brochure, and BRC. Prospects were offered an incentive of a fifty-dollar Gift Card for use at Sharper Image.com in addition to the more business-focused offer. In this way, J.D. Edwards was able to appeal to both the audience's personal and professional sides.

Telemarketing, both inbound and outbound, was used in order to lift response for all other media elements. An inbound 800-number was included as a response mechanism on all outbound communications. In addition, outbound telemarketing was used a follow-up to direct mail and e-mail pushes.

Results

With dedicated 800-numbers, URLs, and coded BRCs, J.D. Edwards tracked response by media touchpoint, providing valuable information for future campaigns.

- The e-mail campaign resulted in 211 responses; which generated thirty-four qualified sales leads.
- The print ads brought in forty-four responses; generating three qualified leads.
- Banner advertising produced 319 click-throughs; resulting in eighteen qualified leads.
- Direct mail produced forty-three responses (representing a response rate of 3.4%, significant for the high level executive audience); and of these, thirty-three were qualified leads.

It is important to remember that the campaign was designed to facilitate multiple, multimedia encounters with every prospect. So, even though the print ads do not appear to have generated as many leads as the more direct-oriented media, they almost certainly contributed to the success of all the efforts, creating a multimedia conversation.

For J.D. Edwards, it proved to be a highly constructive conversation too.

Conversations in Action: Software AG

With billions of technology dollars at stake, business-to-business high tech marketers spend an exorbitant amount of money to reach a finite group of decision-makers.

This is good news if you sell space in high tech trade publications or mailing lists of CIOs. It's bad news if you're trying to break through and generate leads for a relatively unknown company.

That's the challenge faced recently by BB&R Marketing and its client, Software AG.

Situation

In recent years, XML (eXtensible Markup Language) has emerged as the technology standard for web-based transactions. Non-proprietary in nature, XML was developed and is recommended by the World Wide Web Consortium. In layman's terms, XML makes it possible for you to store, retrieve, edit, publish, and exchange information via the web, no matter which platform, application type, programming language, or devices are in use at your end or the other end.

Software AG, based in Darmstadt, Germany, is one of the largest and most highly respected system software companies in the world, with an absolute commitment to open-standard XML.

In February 2001, Software AG hired BB&R Marketing to develop and implement an integrated media program that would essentially launch Software AG's XML technology in the United States. BB&R—a direct marketing agency located in Alexandria Virginia—has particular expertise in the marketing of high-technology products and services. It is the agency which guided IBM's initial entry into direct marketing, and as agency-of-record, produced more than 220 highly successful nationwide and international campaigns that delivered over seventy million dollars in revenues to IBM over a period of five years.

Software AG's partners in this undertaking were IBM and IDC (International Data Corp.).

All information, including all illustration, is reprinted with the permission of BB&R Marketing and Software AG.

Marketing Objectives

For this program, Software AG's objectives were to:

1. Develop a campaign that would position them as the leader in XML technology
2. Overcome the impact of "me too" offerings that cluttered the marketplace
3. Pre-empt the thrust of Oracle who was reportedly preparing to launch a directly competitive product
4. Generate qualified and actionable leads for their sales force

Challenges

While very well known in Europe, Software AG was not particularly prominent in the U.S. The theme or centerpiece of the integrated program would have to be compelling enough to motivate the audience to learn more about a company they might not have heard of.

XML technology had become an overnight "buzzword" in the business community. But, the benefits of the technology itself were not well understood. Higher level executives had a built-in resistance to yet another cash-draining "killer" technology. As an additional challenge, business in general was going through a sharp cutback in IT spending.

Target Audience

The list universe was narrowed to eighteen vertical industries, each segmented according to job responsibility criteria.

Jerry Rendich of BB&R stresses that, "Not enough emphasis can be put on this critical first step because fifty to sixty percent of the success or failure of any mailing can be traced directly to list selection and segmentation. It's only after we're certain we've identified the right audience and know we have a clear picture of their particular "hot buttons" that we start the creative development."

The selected lists included subscribers to *Application Trends Magazine, CIO Magazine, Beyond Computing Magazine* and *XML Journal* plus Software AG's list of tradeshow attendees. These lists were narrowed according to corporate revenues and limited to specific vertical industries:

- Accounting
- Application service provider
- Banking and financial services
- Computer technology manufacturing
- Education
- Healthcare and related services
- Insurance
- Internet and ecommerce
- Legal
- Medical
- Pharmaceutical
- Publishing
- Real estate
- Software development
- Systems integrators
- Technology consultants
- Telecommunications
- Wholesale distributor

Within these industries, names were selected and segmented by level of responsibility:

- Senior corporate level (downward recommenders): CEO, CIO, COO, CFO.
- Executive level, decision-makers (primary target audience): VP, EXVP and/or director of IT, operations, marketing, etc., mostly with P&L responsibility at the enterprise or multi-divisional echelon.
- Managerial level (upward recommenders): those with responsibility for implementation of application development, information, and information technology at the divisional or multi-departmental level.
- Larger integrators and consulting firms (lateral recommenders).
- *XML Journal* subscribers and tradeshow names that could not be segmented by level of responsibility.

Strategy

The main event of the Software AG program was more than a marketing conversation, it was an actual conversation between the company, prospective customers, and industry experts that took place via the web.

Drawing on streaming media techniques that had been developed for the educational and corporate training fields, it was determined that a live, interactive web conference would be the centerpiece of the campaign. This was marketed as a "must attend event" rather than as archived information that could be accessed on the web at one's leisure. It was positioned as a valuable informational service to the business community, as opposed to an opportunity for vendors to sell products.

With the web event as a focal point, an integrated mix of media touches would be used to drive registration and attendance, and then to follow-up with event participants.

Integrated Media Conversation

Mailings deliberately conservative in tone and appearance were created in multiple versions according to the segmentation criteria. Each contained a personalized routing slip to encourage pass-along to colleagues, customers, business partners, suppliers, and so forth. The web conference was promoted heavily via IBM's web site and e-newsletter channels.

Multiple mail formats were developed according to segmentation criteria. A six inch x nine inch package with an informational brochure was mailed to the primary audience, upward recommenders, and lateral recommenders. A smaller, #10 format with a quick-read flyer was sent to the senior level audience, and an oversized postcard with a "Do You Speak XML?" bumper sticker was mailed to tradeshow names and *XML Journal* subscribers whose job responsibilities could not be determined. In addition, the primary audience received a follow-up Western Union-gram mailing one week after the initial mail drop.

Telemarketing was also tested to randomly selected names within the primary audience, but was cut off due to relatively low response levels. E-mail was utilized for retention purposes, but not as a cold marketing tactic.

All registrants were acknowledged immediately by e-mail One week prior to the conference they received an animated Flash reminder, and the day before the conference, an e-mail prompt. Registrants were asked to complete a questionnaire that qualified them as to need/interest, budget availability, level of authority, and timeframe.

Streaming media was employed and, as part of the registration process, the software application necessary to view the event was provided. Each registrant's system was automatically checked to determine their bandwidth capabilities. The event was broadcast simultaneously in several different bandwidths to accommodate those who might opt to participate from home or other locations without high-speed Internet access.

After the event, each participant received an immediate follow-up e-mail and a fulfillment kit with the shape and appearance of a pizza box. Along with the four informational booklets, (illustrated white papers), they received a pizza mouse pad, a pizza cutter, and a ten dollar gift certificate to Pizza Hut.

Software AG and IBM made immediate telephone contact with

Innovative "pizza box" direct mail created a buzz at prospect companies.

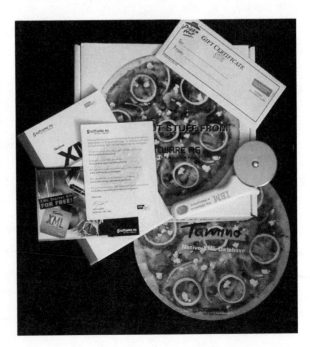

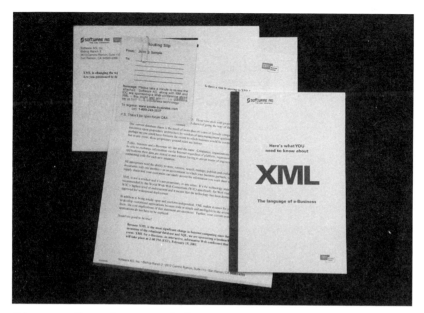

Direct mail packages included an informative booklet on XML technology.

Both electronic and printed collateral carried through the creative theme.

The marketing conversation continued with event collateral.

Flat direct mail was sent via USPS and via Western Union.

participants and registered non-participants. With each sales call appointment, prospects received high-end collateral materials including a CD transcript of the conference to share with colleagues.

A cross-section of non-respondents was re-mailed, promoting the archived version of the web conference; results to this re-mail were marginal.

Implementation Schedule

- Primary mailing—January 15, 2001
- Followup mailing (primary audience only)—January 21, 2001
- E-mail acknowledgement—immediately upon registration
- Flash e-mail promotion—February 8, 2001
- Last-minute reminder (e-mail)—February 13, 2001
- Live web conference—February 15, 2001

Results

Pre-event marketing resulted in a total of 1219 registrants, all of whom were considered qualified leads, of which 633 actually took part in the conference. Interestingly, all 633 stayed online for the entire conference plus the Q&A session that followed the presentations.

Following presentations by industry experts from Software AG, IBM, and IDC, live questions were addressed for the benefit of the entire audience. A total of seventy-two questions were received, all of which were screened on the fly and directed to the appropriate panelists who responded in "real time."

After the event, the sales force was able to secure 330 decision-level sales appointments. Neither IBM nor Software AG discloses actual sales figures. However, at an average close rate of ten to fifteen percent and a product solution that averages nine hundred thousand dollars in price, the estimated sales are between thirty and forty-four million dollars.

The total cost of the campaign including creative, production, the conference itself, and fulfillment was under four hundred thousand dollars, making this a very satisfying conversation for Software AG.

Conversations in Action: SourceLink

If you're reading this book, there's a good chance that you are either practicing or studying direct marketing. So, it probably won't surprise you to learn that direct marketing is big business. In 2001, overall spending for direct marketing initiatives was projected to reach $191.6 billion, up 8.5% from the previous year. In fact, direct marketing expenditures represented more than half—56.5%—of total U.S. advertising expenditures. Securing a bigger piece of this pie was a primary goal for direct marketing companies like SourceLink.

Situation

By 2001, SourceLink was the nation's seventh largest direct marketing organization, having grown through acquisition of smaller best-of-breed agencies and production companies. SourceLink positioned itself as "a single company comprising an integrated array of marketing capabilities and services designed to help you get, keep, and grow profitable customer relationships." But, competition was fierce.

There were many and different types of companies vying for direct marketing projects. In addition to direct marketing firms, there were general ad agencies, print production companies, letter shops, database, and CRM companies and consulting firms. Decision-makers at client companies were literally bombarded with communications from these competing businesses.

SourceLink needed to cut through the abundance of materials that the target audience received from the industry on a daily basis, and also engage them in a long-term conversation.

According to Jim Hackett, SourceLink's Vice President, Business Development, "SourceLink's goal was to build a new business engine that could be used by corporate to generate national accounts or by each location to win local or specialized business."

Although many of SourceLink's locations had been in business for decades, SourceLink as one company was new. The marketing communications program, therefore, had to build the SourceLink brand while it generated demand for services. As with most self-promotion, all of

All information, including all illustration, is reprinted with permission of Jim Hackett, of SourceLink.

this had to be done on a limited budget, with limited resources and in a limited amount of time.

Target Audience

The primary target audience consisted of Vice Presidents and Directors of Marketing in the middle markets, i.e.,companies that were about five hundred million dollars in size. Although SourceLink decided to focus mainly on business-to-business, some business-to-consumer companies were identified in targeted categories. These categories were high technology, telecommunications, and utilities. Companies were further targeted by their propensity to utilize direct marketing.

Secondary targets included SourceLink employees, prospective and current clients, vendors, industry influencers such as industry press and agency search consultants, and prospective and current investors.

Marketing Objectives

The primary objective of Phase One was to generate enough qualified leads to successfully close three to five national accounts, resulting in two million dollars or more in net revenue. The corporate marketing efforts would continue in Phase Two, with the additional objective of providing tools that would enable each location to increase its revenue by five percent.

SourceLink aimed to establish benchmarks against which future communications efforts would be measured, including:

- Response to individual programs—prospect dialogues and meetings, raw response data via inbound 800-numbers, web site hits, BRCs, fax replies
- Revenue generated by new accounts
- Sales force activity—appointments, RFPs, new accounts
- Database updates
- Interactive response data—repeat visits, length of stay, key pages, paths taken
- Response opt-ins or requests for additional information
- Awareness and mindshare

Challenges

SourceLink needed to be as efficient as possible in generating business for both the corporation and the individual locations. Yet the prospect audience, even within targeted industries, was potentially quite large, taking in the number of companies and multiple titles that could be responsive to the message. The solution was to create a hand-built, tele-verified database to minimize waste in both direct marketing communications efforts and selling activities.

Prospects who buy integrated marketing and direct marketing production services need to be presented with a compelling argument or be caught at the right time to get them to consider changing their current set of partners and vendors. Therefore, the plan was to send a steady stream of communications that told the SourceLink story in bite-sized pieces.

Prospects also look to reduce the risk of their decision by assessing a combination of each agency's reputation, client list, and personal and professional references. A decision was made to provide ample case histories in presentation material and on the web site.

Marketing Communications Plan

The plan included two phases. The main purpose of the first phase was to generate immediate sales activity so that SourceLink and each individual location could pursue leads, close sales, and win business. The second phase was designed to support both the corporate and individual location sales forces going forward by providing a "toolkit" of proven lead generation and relationship marketing vehicles.

The marketing communications plan included a variety of integrated media activities in order to introduce the company, engage the prospective client, and build an ongoing conversation. Throughout, there were many opportunities for the prospect to say "yes." This was to be accomplished by frequent, sequenced touches, driven from a well-maintained prospect database, each having a single focus.

By keeping individual touches single-minded, each point would have a better chance to register. The prospect would receive the "whole story" one bite-sized chunk at a time until a critical mass of awareness and perception of SourceLink's solution would be realized. By varying the media and types of touches, a composite perception would be created quickly. By including response vehicles and telemarketing, the prospect data would be updated. This process was designed to yield new prospects and eliminate waste. Having been tested and refined in the field, these marketing components would be made available to individual SourceLink locations.

Creative

Although most of the media chosen was direct response in nature, establishing a brand for SourceLink was an important objective of the campaign. In addition, the target audience was media-savvy and sophisticated. For both these reasons, a truly engaging creative theme was critical to the program's success. The agency needed a way to demonstrate the true value of its collective wisdom. The solution was "Marketology."

Marketology was defined as "A new branch of learning that focuses in how to get, keep, and grow profitable customer relationships." It was brought to life by a card deck that offered sixty-two cards in four suits that dramatized the stages of building an effective direct marketing campaign: The Hunter, The Builder, The Muse, and The Surveyor.

"I collect antique tarot decks," explained Creative Director Walter Charles Bumford III. "They provided a lot of inspiration. Of course, we chose to update the graphics, give them a "cyber" edge, to appeal to a modern audience."

Billed as "Your journey to a higher marketing consciousness," the Marketology card deck offered tips and exercises that brought clients closer to the art and science of all media direct marketing. It was also designed to have a long "shelf life" at the prospective client's office.

An Integrated Conversation

With a creative theme that was unique and engaging, and an offer that allowed prospects to test-drive the agency's thinking, SourceLink launched an integrated media conversation. Phase One components included:

A custom 3-D package included the Marketology *card deck.*

- Outbound telemarketing. Each of the targeted companies was called and televerified, ensuring a highly accurate list.
- Teaser e-mail campaign. This enabled SourceLink to test the idea of the card deck before committing to it. And, because e-mail is quick to implement, they could get the message out without waiting for the Marketology card deck to be produced.
- "Taste" web site, a temporary site, designed as a linear "slideshow," was set up to handle inquiries while a full-scale site was in production.
- Flat mail. Sample cards were sent in a square vellum envelope with an offer for the complete card deck.
- Card deck fulfillment. Housed in a presentation box, the card deck was sent Priority Mail or, in the case of hot prospects, hand-delivered.
- Three -D mail to select targets. The most promising prospects were sent the card deck in lieu of the flat mail package.
- Follow-up telemarketing. Everyone who received a card deck was called by one of SourceLink's sales reps.

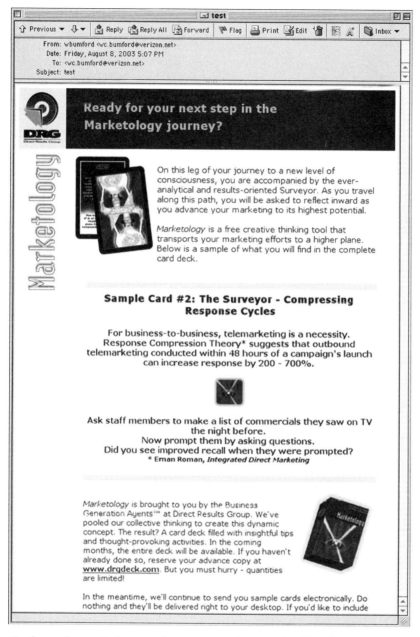

Outbound email began the conversation and offered a "taste" of Marketology.

Phase Two communications included refined versions of all of the above as well as:

- Expanded web site. Enhanced with case studies and more detailed information, the web site was designed for self-navigation, or as a presentation aid for sales reps.
- Print ads for individual locations. A print ad that offered the Marketology card deck was developed so that SourceLink locations could take advantage of local media opportunities.
- E-mail campaigns. A rich html e-mail series was developed that offered the "Marketology" card deck, while positioning SourceLink as a happy alternative to other agencies.
- Collateral. New presentation materials were created for the corporate sell and templates and tools were generated for the individual locations.
- Branding. "Elevator Talk" pieces were written that were concise, easy-to comprehend, and demonstrated SourceLink's capabilities and benefits. A version for corporate major accounts and a related version for each location were created.

Results

The inbound response rate from the integrated campaign was 11.3 %. In addition to engaging dozens of qualified prospects in conversation, the program also resulted in five new major accounts and more than six million dollars in agency billings.

The Marketology integrated campaign was recognized with two Gold Echo Awards by the Direct Marketing Association.

Conversations in Action: Technology Review

Throughout this book, we've emphasized the importance of understanding your target audience. This becomes a particularly valuable tool when your knowledge goes beyond demographic data and moves into your audience's behavior, attitudes, and inner vision.

Here's a case study that illustrates just how effective your marketing conversation can be when you know how to talk to your audience, and exactly how and where to reach them through integrated media.

It's a subscriber acquisition campaign for *Technology Review*, developed and implemented by direct marketing agency Passaic Parc.

Situation

Since 1999, *Technology Review* has been the Massachusetts Institute of Technology's (MIT) magazine of innovation. Its mission statement reads, "To promote the understanding of emerging technologies and their impact on leaders." The magazine is published ten times a year and basic subscriptions are thirty-four dollars.

Technology Review has been a success story. With a current circulation of 315,000, *Technology Review* has increased circulation over 235% in the past three years.

However, as with all publications, the key to *Technology Review's* continued stability and growth is new subscriber acquisition. Results for the publication's control package had decreased for the past three years.

Agency Passaic Parc was charged with developing and implementing a campaign that would bring results back up and give *Technology Review* new and proven communications tools for future efforts.

Target Audience

The average reader of *Technology Review* is male, aged forty-eight, with a household income of two hundred and eight thousand dollars , and a net worth of $1.7 million.

They are considered "thought-leaders" and are, predominantly,

- Senior executives
- Well-educated
- And, pre-disposed to applying innovative technology to reach business objectives

Robert Rosenthal, President of Passaic Parc, described the target audience as the "technological intelligentsia. Leaders in spheres of science, engineering, business, and investment."

In its media kit, *Technology Review* describes its audience as,

"People who understand what the future holds, people who appreciate the power of technology's role in business and society, and have long been the drivers of the global economy. They invent new products, create new industries, and read Technology Review. For our audience, knowledge is power and Technology Review delivers."

This is a great descriptive profile and would prove valuable to the creative team, but the trick was to use this "soft" data to drive "hard data," like list selection.

Marketing Objectives

The primary objective was to cost-effectively build awareness and acquire new subscriptions. In doing so, the program would have to "beat the control."

Additionally, client and agency wanted to gain learning about the effectiveness of an integrated media approach. So, testing would be built into each touchpoint of the campaign.

Challenges

The audience receives frequent communications and offers from business and technology publications. The campaign had to stand out and generate results on a relatively low budget.

And, as stated above, it's easy to describe the ideal *Technology Review* reader, but it's more difficult to pinpoint who they are and how to reach them.

Strategy

The offer for this program was two free issues. The rationale was that prospective subscribers would recognize the value of the publication by trying it for themselves. And, this created synergy with the offer posted on www.technologyreview.com.

A decision was made to utilize direct mail and e-mail in concert. The audience is technologically-savvy and comfortable with e-mail. And, it was assumed that the two media, working together, would lift the response of each individual tactic.

Finally, a decision was made to mail packages to the prospects' homes rather than their places of business. This would decrease the amount of "clutter" the mail would have to break through. There would be fewer "gatekeepers" who might throw away a solicitation. The team was not concerned about speaking to this audience regarding business issues while they were in their homes. After all, the audience was made up of people who eat, sleep, and breathe business and technology.

Creative and Messaging

Rosenthal explains the process, "We developed unusual concepts tied to the underlying greatness of the publication." Consequently, Rosenthal's creative team worked with *Technology Review's* actual content to generate ideas for the campaign.

In an e-mail touchpoint, for example, the headline reads, "Is this where computing's next breakthrough will come from?" with a photo of a lab beaker. The intriguing question leads recipients to a link that takes them to the www.technologyreview.com web site, where they get the full story and a taste of the magazine's aforementioned, "greatness."

An Integrated Conversation

The program began with e-mail blasts delivered to two hundred thousand prospects. Half of these were from a house list of people who had subscribed to *Technology Review's* e-newsletters, but not to the magazine itself. The remaining one hundred thousand e-mail addresses were rented.

Direct mail packages, including a letter, brochure, and BRC, were sent to eight hundred thousand names rented from other publications and compiled lists. Creative was tested in order to establish a new control package.

"A special invitation from MIT: R.S.V.P. by February 1, 2002." proved

Personalized response mechanism offered free issues and online access.

Creative theme tapped into the personality of Technology Review *subscribers.*

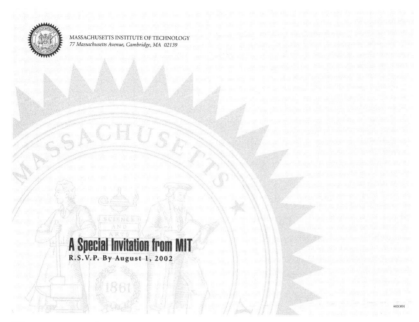

MASSACHUSETTS INSTITUTE OF TECHNOLOGY
77 Massachusetts Avenue, Cambridge, MA 02139

A Special Invitation from MIT
R.S.V.P. By August 1, 2002

The outer envelope leveraged the publication's affiliation with M.I.T.

Free **unlimited** online **access** to
Technology Review archives.

With your paid subscription, you gain access to hundreds of *Technology Review* articles from the past five years, searchable by keyword. Recent articles include:

- *Handhelds of Tomorrow*
- *Why Missile Defense Won't Work*
- *Economic Bust, Patent Boom*
- *Nanobiotech Makes the Diagnosis*
- *Motorola's Superchip*
- *A.I. Reboots*
- *Merck's Mission: An AIDS Vaccine*
- *Getting Over Oil*
- *Whose Nuclear Waste?*
- *DNA Chips Target Cancer*
- *A Smarter Power Grid*
- *The Nanotube Computer*

- *Detecting Bioterrorism*
- *The Next Computer Interface*
- *Lean Mean R&D Machines*
- *The Future of TV*
- *A Fuel Cell in Your Phone*
- *New Life for DuPont*
- *Speeding Drug Discovery*
- *It's Time for Clockless Chips*
- *DARPA's Disruptive Technologies*
- *The Proteomics Payoff*
- *Brain Pacemakers*
- *Beyond the Bar Code*

MIT'S MAGAZINE OF INNOVATION
TECHNOLOGY
Where emerging technologies emerge

A buckslip highlighted the online features of subscription.

to be the winning teaser copy on the outer envelope. The creative strategy behind the winning package, like the strategy that drove the e-mail, was to highlight the magazine's editorial.

Results

In order to gain knowledge that would drive future efforts, the team tracked overall response as well as results from each tactical execution.

E-mail response was considerably higher than industry average and also higher than past efforts for *Technology Review*. The "Beaker" e-mail pulled an extremely high net response rate of 6.5%. This represents total trial subscriptions as a percentage of total e-mail quantity. This execution beat a previous e-mail response record by thirty-one percent.

Many lists were tested for direct mail. The best performers were professional associations; paid publications in categories such as consumer science; and upscale newsletter lists.

The net response rate on the "Sheet of Glass" direct mail was improved by more than twenty one percent, and became the highest net response rate in the history of the magazine. So, the increase was significant.

Technology Review Inc.'s Martha Connors, Vice President and General Manager asserted, "That's a huge lift for us."

Just how huge is huge? Elaine Spencer, Director of Consumer Marketing at *Technology Review*, recently explained that with the higher response rate, "We've saved in the range of the mid six figures."

Now, that *is* huge.

Conversations in Action: Washington Post

Imagine yourself in your industry's "pole position," with more than fifty percent of the available market loyal to your product and the closest competitor operating with only one-eighth the number of customers. Most companies dream of saturating a market. With that success comes a different kind of challenge. How do you continue to grow?

Situation

Since it first began publication over a century ago, *The Washington Post* has evolved into one of the most recognized news organizations in the world. Each week *The Post's* Circulation Department oversees delivery of over five million newspapers to homes, businesses, and news racks. *The Post* is an operating division of The Washington Post Company and employs about three thousand people.

The average daily issue of *The Post* is read by fifty-three percent of the Washington D.C. Metro Market and the average Sunday issue is read by sixty-seven percent. In comparison, *The Washington Times* is read by only seven percent.

However, despite *The Post's* clear leadership position, trends over the last five years showed declining subscriptions. To address this, the marketing team at *The Post* had developed a creative theme, "$20.03 in 2003." *The Post's* typical offer was eight weeks. This was a six-month offer.

Silver Marketing in Bethesda, Maryland was challenged to come up with a winning program to promote the new subscription offer.

Marketing Objectives

The Post hoped to achieve several objectives with the program:

- Grow Sunday circulation
- Reinforce brand relevance and value to drive readership— every day
- Acquire new subscribers
- Upgrade existing subscribers
- Improve subscription retention

- Strengthen *The Post's* position among high growth/ opportunity markets

Target Audience

The majority of the target audience is educated, busy, and has many demands on their time. Among readers, there is a high degree of loyalty.

However, the marketplace also has a high degree of transients and therefore needs to be replaced constantly. "New Movers" were a prime target.

In addition, because *The Post* was interested in establishing relationships with long-term potential, an important subset of the audience was young adults.

Secondary prospects were current Sunday-only subscribers. The objective was to motivate them to upgrade to daily delivery.

Challenges

The Post had nearly saturated the market in the D.C. metro area, and the largest client-supplied file had historically performed poorly. So, finding effective new lists in large enough quantities posed a great challenge.

Creatively, the team also would be challenged to develop an effective theme that could be applied to everything from direct mail and *The Post's* web site to individual promotional items, like balloons and stickers.

A final challenge faced by the team was timing. Developing the program creative strategy, copywriting and designing, data processing, printing, producing, and mailing would coincide with three holidays, Thanksgiving, Christmas, and New Year's. This would require efficiency on the part of the agency. It also meant that the message would have to work harder in order to gain attention and resonate with prospective subscribers during the busy holiday season.

Strategy

An important element of the strategy was re-positioning *The Post's* offer so that it would communicate a clear benefit to prospective subscribers. Instead of telling them what they would *pay* ("$20.03 in 2003"), the recommended messaging explained what they would *save*

("Save 44%!"). This is a good example of focusing on the customer's needs rather than a clever creative solution.

The team determined that a multimedia launch of the new offer would capture any "low hanging fruit" and create the greatest demand as quickly as possible. For both effectiveness and efficiency, a decision was made to utilize the following mix of media:

- Direct mail
- Single-copy inserts
- Door hangers
- A custom promotional wrap for the papers

In order to create synergy at every point of the distribution chain, budget was allocated to include and motivate distributors, staff, and field sales representatives.

Finally, the team focused on testing rented lists in order to improve upon the results *The Post* was experiencing using its house file.

Implementation

An engaging creative theme was developed to tie-in with the holiday season and to communicate that this was a new and different offer from *The Post*. The theme, "New Year New Deal" came to life in bright, bold colors and graphics that were flexible enough to use in a variety of media and on a variety of substrates.

Direct mail reached 317,945 prospects at a total budget cost of $137,156 including creative, list, mailing, DP, postage, and all professional service/agency fees. The eye-catching package included a bright yellow envelope with the bold red and black "New Year New Deal" mark. A sticker was added to the envelope as an involvement device to be placed on the response mechanism. And, strong benefit messages and an emphasis on savings throughout the year (with coupons etc.) drove the copy.

The same colors and graphics were used on door hangers, newspaper inserts and wraps. In every case, the offer was the "hero" of the communications. A prominent, red 800-number and *The Washington Post's* URL were highlighted to drive response.

Graphics were applied across media to build a cohesive marketing conversation.

Recognizing that *The Post's* internal audience could help make the program a greater success, a creative solution was developed to involve them emotionally as well. Jelly bean-filled champagne bottles, with custom "New Year New Deal" labels, were given to distributors, staff, and the field to encourage buy-in and to further promote the new offer.

Results

For the mailing, *The Post* received 3,497 responses—equating to 1.1%—extremely high given the mass-market nature of the product category and its current saturation of the marketplace. The average response rate for the previous year's campaigns was .6% so this represented a considerable improvement. In fact, the new program lifted response by eighty-three percent.The cost per lead was $39.22.

And, the extensive list testing uncovered lists options that outperformed *The Post's* house list by three hundred percent.

For *The Washington Post*, the integrated media conversation, "New Year New Deal," proved that, even when you're at the top, there's still room to grow. And, the program was recognized with a Gold Maxi by the DMAW.

About the Authors

DONNA BAIER STEIN has been a direct marketing copywriter for 25 years, working for publishers, associations, consumer and business-to-business clients, including American Express, Sprint, Travel & Leisure, GEICO, Fidelity, AARP, Time-Life, Physicians for Social Responsibility, the Smithsonian Institution, World Wildlife Fund, Eating Well Magazine, MIT Technology Review, Beech Aircraft, Arthur Andersen & Company, Hallmark Cards, IBM and many others. Her work has won CAPLES, MAXI, AMBIT and other awards.

Donna has served on the Board of Directors of the Direct Marketing Association of Washington (DMAW), co-founded the DMAW Creative Council, and was President of the New England Direct Marketing Association. She is currently a member of the Direct Marketing Idea Exchange.

She is a frequent lecturer on direct marketing and copywriting and is an Adjunct Professor at both New York University and Fairleigh Dickinson University. She has also taught at the University of Missouri at Kansas City professional certification program in direct marketing, Virginia Commonwealth University DM certification program, Johns Hopkins University, Gotham Writers Workshop, The American University, and many regional DM clubs and conferences including New England Publishing Day, Society of National Association Publications, Nonprofits in Travel, etc. She gives seminars around the country on copywriting and winning direct mail for the national Direct Marketing Association. She also gives in-house seminars for companies that include Fidelity, AT&T, Physicians Mutual Insurance Company, and others.

Donna's book on direct mail copywriting, Write on Target!, which she co-authored with Floyd Kemske, was published in 1997 by NTC Publishing Group. It is in wide use in university and college marketing programs and also among DM practitioners. In addition, she has received a fellowship from The Writing Seminars at The Johns Hopkins University, a scholarship from Bread Loaf Writers Conference, and other awards for fiction and poetry. Her novel, Fortune, received the PEN/New England Discovery Award for Fiction. In 2003, she was named the Direct Marketer of the Year by the New England Direct Marketing Association.

She is President of Baier Stein Direct, www.directcopy.com.

Alexandra MacAaron is Executive Vice President, Chief Operations Officer and Executive Creative Director As EVP/COO/ECD, Alex demonstrates her enthusiasm for the alphabet. Alex also leads the coordinated efforts of creative, production, interactive and account service on all client business, including SpeechWorks, Forrester Research, Eddie Bauer, Bay State Gas, Bell Atlantic, GTE Internetworking and Saucony Footwear. She brings with her nearly two decades of experience in direct marketing, advertising and new media communications in Boston and New York.

Prior to joining Direct Results Group/SourceLink, Alex was Vice President/Creative Director for Berenson, Isham & Partners; and Redgate Communications; and Associate Creative Director at Continental Cablevision. Over the years, she has developed and implemented integrated marketing campaigns for clients such as Polaroid, Club Med, NYNEX, Stride Rite, HBO and Chevrolet. Earlier in her career, she served as copywriter on numerous accounts, including Sony, General Electric and Simon & Schuster. More recently, Alex launched Cuneo Direct, the direct marketing division of Cuneo Sullivan Dolabany.

Alex is the recipient of dozens of advertising industry awards, including numerous regional awards as well as national/international honors such as 3 DMA Gold ECHO Awards; the BPME Gold Award for Broadcast Promotion; and the "Best of Show" Silver Microphone award for a jingle package. She has taught at several local universities and frequently lectures for various New England associations.

She is also the Vice President of the New England Direct Marketing Association and is Chairperson of NEDMA's Annual Conference.

Index